WOW! What a great, easy to read business book. *The First 2 Hours* is overflowing with great insights and practical advice to make sure you truly do get the most out of your day.

— **Gabrielle Dolan**, Global expert on
business storytelling and
author of *Stories for Work* and *Real Communication*

I am a massive fan of Donna's two-part pragmatism and inspiration and *The First 2 Hours* meets all my expectations and then some. If you want an upgrade around how you live and do life then get your hot little hands on this one. You can't afford not to.

— **Georgia Murch**, Author and
keynote speaker

Many workplaces I go into are chock full of people blearily staring at screens in the morning, stressed and overwhelmed with the amount of work to be done. Donna's book *The First 2 Hours* is jam packed full of pragmatic ways to change that. Giving us the lens of when rather than what, Donna turns what we do with our day on its head. Donna's approach to how we use our time more effectively is accessible, doable and practical. The research is fascinating, as are the simple ways we can save ourselves from the crushing vortex of 'busyness fatigue'. Along with Donna's previous book *The 25 Minute Meeting*, *The First 2 Hours* is a game changer.

— **Tracey Ezard**, Professional Triber,
Learning Culture expert, speaker, facilitator and
author of *Glue* and *The Buzz*

Imagine that there were ways to set ourselves up to have awesomely productive days every day—rather than those days where we are struggling to get through our to do list, and find ourselves spending hours outside of work getting our work done. Donna has written a deceptively simple book and shows how, with a few tweaks to our day, we can tap into our energy levels and work so much more productively and enjoyably. Donna continues to set the benchmark for helping us manage our productivity and time, first with *The 25 Minute Meeting* and now with *The First 2 Hours*. If you are looking for a practical, evidence-based guide to help you design your day and take back control of your life, you must read this.

—**Maree Burgess,** Trainer, executive coach, facilitator and author of *The XX Project* and *Connecting Us*

With much written about being our best, working at our optimum, needing more sleep and the problems with multi-tasking, *The First 2 Hours* gathers, presents and explains the leading thinking on what we need to be doing with the most important time of our day. Tasks, activities, self-assessments and tips, combine with practical advice that can be implemented immediately. Leaders and teams in organisations would do well to adopt the advice here to make significant gains personally and professionally. It's time to stop fighting for productivity and start going with the elements that science, experience, research and data say will help us truly be our best. Aaaaah … it feels better already.

—**Lynne Cazaly,** Speaker, author and facilitator

THE FIRST 2 HOURS

THE FIRST 2 HOURS

MAKE BETTER USE OF YOUR MOST VALUABLE TIME

DONNA McGEORGE

WILEY

First published in 2019 by John Wiley & Sons Australia, Ltd

42 McDougall St, Milton Qld 4064

Office also in Melbourne

Typeset in 12/15pt Bembo Std

© John Wiley & Sons Australia, Ltd 2019

The moral rights of the author have been asserted

A catalogue record for this book is available from the National Library of Australia

Cover design by Wiley

Cover image © Rashad Ashur / Shutterstock

Printed in Singapore by C.O.S. Printers Pte Ltd

10 9 8 7 6 5 4 3 2 1

Disclaimer

The material in this publication is of the nature of general comment only, and does not represent professional advice. It is not intended to provide specific guidance for particular circumstances and it should not be relied on as the basis for any decision to take action or not take action on any matter which it covers. Readers should obtain professional advice where appropriate, before making any such decision. To the maximum extent permitted by law, the author and publisher disclaim all responsibility and liability to any person, arising directly or indirectly from any person taking or not taking action based on the information in this publication.

Contents

About the author

Donna McGeorge makes work *work*.

She is passionate about enhancing the large amount of time we spend in our workplace (too much, for many) to ensure it is effective and productive, as well as enjoyable.

Donna has worked with managers and leaders throughout Australia and the Asia–Pacific for over 20 years. She delivers practical skills, training, workshops and facilitation to corporates—such as Nissan Motor Company, Jetstar, Medibank Private and Ford Motor Company—so they learn to manage their people well and produce great performance and results.

Her CV is as eclectic as her record collection (yes, classic vinyl). In addition to roles at Telstra, Qantas, Ernst & Young and Ansett, she has been Manager of Theatre, Sports & Concert Tours for the UK-based Keith Prowse, and Asia–Pacific Organisational Development Manager for Ford Motor Company in Shanghai, China.

Donna also shares her knowledge for good, writing articles for the likes of *The Age, Smart Company, B&T, HRM*, and other publications. *The First 2 Hours* is her second book; *The 25 Minute Meeting*, her first book, was published by John Wiley & Sons in 2018.

She runs her business from 20 acres in Heathcote, Victoria, a region known for its world-class shiraz, but her most creative moments come while sipping tea on her verandah and gazing at the rolling hills alongside her husband, Steve, and dog, Prudence.

Donna believes that workplaces are complex, but not hard to get on track. More often than not it's getting the simple things right, consistently, that has the greatest impact.

She also knows that when we decide to be intentional, we can surprise ourselves with what we can achieve. Read on and you'll soon see.

www.donnamcgeorge.com

Acknowledgements

In 2018, I published my first 'proper' book, *The 25 Minute Meeting*. It was a super steep learning curve and I couldn't have done it without the team that supported me. Now here I am in 2019, publishing my second book (can you imagine?) and, yet again, it has been another team effort.

Thank you to my friends at Wiley—Lucy, for having faith in doing the second book before we saw how the sales for the first would be. Ingrid for answering any and all questions with such patience and forbearance. Peter and the marketing team for getting my books into stores and positioned to their best advantage.

Kelly Irving—legend. You demystify every part of writing a book, and break it down into digestible chunks that not only make the process fluid and manageable, but downright enjoyable. With each book our relationship deepens, making working with you just like hanging out with a mate.

The Brains Trust—I love the fires of creation we spark every time we hang out together. Whenever I need anything, I need simply ask. You gals always have my back, and I'm lucky to have you. Thank you Maree Burgess, Tracey Ezard, Lynne Cazaly and Deb Dalziel.

Anne-Marie Johnson—we've known each other for so long that when I put my manuscript in your hands I know I'm going to get no-nonsense, nothing-but-the-truth feedback. I have come to love and trust your expertise in the Queen's English. Thank you also for rearranging books in bookstores so mine are front and centre.

Alexandra Martindale—writing this book took a greater toll on the business than I intended. Your patience with me while I worked through it and got on the other side of it has been nothing short of phenomenal. I'm so grateful to have you in my life.

Emma McGeorge—you continue to be the inspiration for much of my writing as I strive to create a better corporate working environment for everyone, and, particularly, for you. I love you my darling girl.

And finally, there is NOTHING I could do in my professional or personal life without the loving support of my husband, Steve. Nothing has changed since the last time I wrote acknowledgements for a book. You are still of service. You still swap out empty cups of tea and bring me snacks without me noticing. I'm still blessed. Thank you, my love.

Introduction

The alarm goes off and you jump out of bed towards the bathroom. You splash some water on your face and stare at your wardrobe trying to think of what to wear to the office. Wait—no time for that, you're going to miss your train!

The next hour is a blur of carparks and kid drop-offs. When you finally get to sit down on your commute, you open up your laptop and are horrified to see 100-plus new emails have pinged into your inbox.

In the following 30 minutes, you manage to delete 27 newsletters, reject 11 meeting invites and respond in detail to just two emails. It's only 8.30 am and your brain is fried.

By the time you get to the office you are *exhausted*, not to mention 10 minutes late to your first meeting.

Unfortunately, scenarios like this are all too common for all too many people.

We start off our day on the wrong foot, stressed and rushing for the door, only to open up our computers and be inundated with requests from other people and actions that take us away from our most valuable tasks for the day.

How can we expect to get a valuable day's work done if we start it by reacting to whatever is in our inbox or whoever is at our desk?

You're stuck in a vicious cycle: starting the day tired, doing the best you can through to the afternoon, working late, going home grumpy and then waking up the next morning to start the cycle all over again.

To try and fix the problem, you've been to endless time management courses and read all the productivity books in the world. Yet still, nothing seems to be working. The volume of your work is ever increasing, and you are now being asked to do more with less—I mean, c'mon!

The problem is that traditional time management theories haven't kept pace with modern workplace demands.

They focus too much on the *what* of our work. They require us to list all the tasks we need to do, then prioritise them according to what is most urgent and important—but what if *all* of your work is urgent and important?

We need to focus less on *what* we do, and more on *when* we do it.

In his book *The Power of Habit,* Charles Duhigg explains that there are things that we can do upon waking that have a positive impact on our mental and physical wellbeing throughout the day. The same can be said for the habits we have in the first two hours of our working day.

There are things we are currently doing when we arrive at the office that drag us and our productivity down for the *entire day*: checking our inbox, tidying our desk, responding to 'urgent' queries, discussing the football scores from the weekend or the latest exit from our favourite reality show. Sure, these things still hold a place in the day, but is first thing the best time to do them? That's the question this book will answer.

What if I told you there are particular tasks that, if done first thing, would actually *add* value to your role and to your whole day?

Before you throw this book away in horror at the thought of not being able to grab a coffee on the way into work (I would never advocate that), what we're talking about here is understanding that our mind and body have innate cycles that can help or hinder our productivity at certain times of the day.

What you're about to discover is that there are optimum times for doing certain types of work — responding to emails, conducting meetings, devising next year's strategy — not just in the first two hours of your day, but at all hours of the workday until home time.

So, while the first two hours of your day is important, the work doesn't stop there.

Fortunately, the first two hours have a flow-on effect, so by understanding when you're most alert or when you need some down time, and marrying that with the tasks you've got to do, you can become more productive. You can take yourself off autopilot and take back control of every hour of your day, doing the right work at the right time (even if you consider yourself a night owl).

You're going to learn how to work with your natural rhythms, not against them, to fuel your productivity.

Just by making some small changes to our habits at specific times of the day, we can set ourselves up to be more efficient, effective and, well, happy!

The old adage of working smarter, not harder, is what is at play here. You will learn to make conscious choices about what you need to do, and then decide the best time to do it.

It's time to set yourself up for success with a different way of working throughout your day.

Ready?

Personal Productivity Quiz

Before we get started, it's important to get an understanding of what your current workday habits are.

Take this quick quiz, originally developed by the team at the blog I Done This and adapted with permission for use here.

Read the questions and circle the answer you feel sounds most like you. Be honest now, no cheating!

1. What do you generally do in the first two hours of your day?

    A Drink coffee. I can't do or think about anything until I have had my coffee.

    B Check my emails and start replying to them all before realising I was meant to be in a meeting five minutes ago.

C Check my emails, answer most of them immediately, then make a comprehensive to-do list that makes me feel immediately stressed.

D Check my emails, answer a couple, and then shut down my inbox and start on the day's most pressing tasks.

E Scan my email, and schedule time to respond to anything urgent or those that need a comprehensive answer. Check my schedule. Plan my day around what I want to achieve by the end.

2. When you get an unexpected project with a tight deadline, how do you feel?

A Totally flustered! It's not my fault that others can't get their act together.

B Okay. If my boss says it has to get done, I'll do it.

C Pumped! I love working fast against a deadline.

D Surprised but I'm ready for it. I like doing what needs to get done.

E Ready. I have a few things I need to shift around, but because I am generally on top of things, I can accommodate last-minute requests.

3. Your boss walks over to your desk on Monday with a long list of tasks due at the end of the week. What are you thinking?

A Seriously?! This is why I can never get on top of my own work.

(Continued)

Personal Productivity Quiz *(cont'd)*

B I'll drop everything and start on them right away.

C I'll add them to my already packed to-do list.

D Sure. I'll check out what needs to be done and work around that and/or do them later.

E All right. I already have time for my most important things blocked out. I'll double check with the boss on the timing and prioritise them according to my schedule.

4. What's your favourite part of the workday?

   A When I get to go home and eat dinner.

   B Don't really have one, any time I get a break I suppose.

   C Late afternoon. I feel the pressure of home time looming and that's when I get most of my work done.

   D Right after lunch. I feel so refreshed!

   E The morning, when I'm getting organised for the day.

5. Oh no! It's Wednesday, and you've just woken up with a stomach virus. Other than being physically ill, how do you feel?

   A Justified. This is what happens when you are overworked.

   B I'm sick. I should stay home. Plus, the day off from work is nice.

   C Nervous and frustrated! It's going to be impossible to finish my to-do list.

D A little worried—I put off a lot to the end of the week, but I'll be able to get it done Thursday and Friday.

E Sick days are unfortunate but necessary. I'll be a little behind, but it's okay—that's why I stay on top of things.

6. On Monday, you have a day-long retreat from work. Instead of doing your job, you're going to be doing 'team-building activities' with your co-workers. How do you feel?

A Ugh! This will interfere with my 'real' work.

B Secretly excited. I get really invested in games.

C Nervous. It sounds like a good idea, but can I afford to lose a whole day?

D A little iffy on games, but if it will help the team.

E Looking forward to it. It's important to take time out from to work on our relationships and the bigger picture.

7. How do you behave in company meetings?

A Zone out. Most of our meetings are a waste of time.

B Try and stay focused while checking my email.

C Act as the meeting's scribe. After the meeting, I send out a comprehensive email, so everyone knows what they're responsible for.

D Take relevant notes and participate where necessary.

E Stay present. If it was important enough for me to accept and attend, I need to see how I can give and get value.

(Continued)

Personal Productivity Quiz *(cont'd)*

8. When do you drink caffeine?

   A All day, every day.

   B Whenever I really need that extra boost to get on my game.

   C Usually twice per day, at regularly scheduled times. Once in the morning and once in the afternoon.

   D In the morning. Occasionally a cup in the afternoon if it's a busy day.

   E When I feel like a treat and only as coffee. It's the thing I use to incentivise myself when I need a little more motivation.

9. You and your co-worker decide you need to set up a meeting with a client. What do you do?

   A Let your co-worker set up the meeting and accept it irrespective of what other meetings you have on. You can decide on the day the most important meeting to attend.

   B Let your co-worker set up the meeting, and then find a way to work around it if it conflicts with something else.

   C Let your co-worker set up a calendar invite. Then, the day of the meeting, prepare extensively.

   D Agree who will send the calendar invite. Then, prepare for the meeting and meet with your co-worker briefly to ensure you're on the same page.

E Send the calendar invite to set up the meeting, along with an email detailing the meeting agenda. Then, schedule time to prepare for the meeting itself.

10. What kind of worker would you describe yourself as? (Be honest, please...)

   A I do what is required but often find demands are unreasonable.

   B I always do my work, but it takes a lot of late nights.

   C I do the job well, but I have a hard time caring about it sometimes.

   D I stay pretty on top of things, but it becomes increasingly harder the more tasks that are dished out.

   E I am immensely organised. I am one of those sickening people who have colour-coded binders for projects, always keep their calendar up to date and use the diary handed out at the beginning of the year to track tasks.

Now tally up your results to see which letter you responded to most and see where you sit on the Deny to Design framework, as shown in figure A (overleaf).

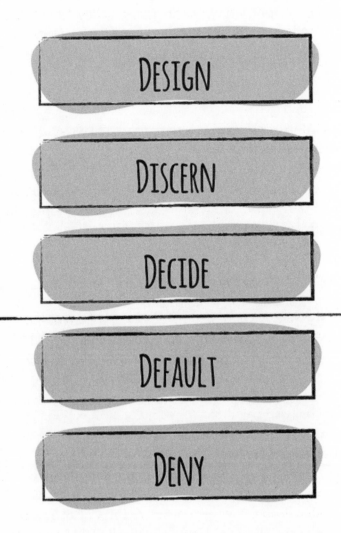

Figure A: the Deny to Design framework

MOSTLY A = DENY

'It's nothing to do with my productivity. It's the amount of work I have, or my boss, or my colleagues. There just isn't enough time in the day to get everything done.'

The funny thing about time is that everyone has the same amount, and yet some people seem to do so much better with what they have. In many respects it's like money. There are some people who earn relatively low salaries and still manage to build wealth and property portfolios. Then there are others who earn relatively *huge* salaries and don't have much to show for it. The feeling here is one of **helplessness** or **hopelessness**.

MOSTLY B = DEFAULT

'My work is controlled by others and I am at the mercy of my calendar and my workload. Shifting deadlines and demands of others determine my priorities.'

You are operating without any thought or direction. You are at the mercy of other people and their most important things. You don't think of your calendar as a resource, but as simply a way to keep track of all the appointments you have. It's likely that you are responding to things in a very reactive and unconsidered way. You experience feelings of **overwhelm**. You get to the end of a day or week and feel like you have been busy, but not productive.

MOSTLY C = DECIDE

'There has to be a better way. Perhaps I need to do a time management course!'

You realise that there is a different and better way of doing the work but have not yet figured it out. You try all sorts of time management or productivity courses but never seem to quite get there, as old habits are hard to break and new habits are hard to form. Often at this level we feel **fatigue**.

MOSTLY D = DISCERN

'Do I really have to be there or do that?'

You are getting there. You will be accepting meeting requests from others, but you are beginning to ask the question 'Do I really need to be there?' 'Is this work I really should be doing?' You are also starting to implement and see results from thinking and working more systematically. For example, you are using your email, calendar and tasks in a more integrated way, and starting to feel the benefits of that. We are starting to feel **hopeful**.

MOSTLY E = DESIGN

'I choose what I do, when I do it and how I do it. I'm still responsive to the needs of others and I am able to manage my workload effectively.'

You are the master of your domain! You use your calendar as a work resource and you allocate time accordingly. You choose what you do and when, and you feel under control.

You truly have life by design. You are clear on your priorities and you are able to make sound choices about what meetings you accept, what activities you undertake and with whom you spend your time. You likely feel **calm**, **centred** and **in control** most of the time.

§ § §

Unless you ticked E for each and every question, it's highly likely that you need to take some immediate action to improve how you prioritise and plan your work and your day. Good job you're here!

Let's help you do that—now.

How to use this book

This book mimics the way I run my workshops, corporate programs and hands-on sessions. It is practical and easy to read and navigate, so you can implement real, but simple, changes to the way you work.

This book is not designed to be a hefty tome you have trouble carrying around, or to be left on your bedside table to gather coffee-cup stains.

Rather, it has quick tips, real-life stories, lots of no-nonsense advice, questions to encourage you to reflect on how you're working now and how you could improve, and exercises to help you implement those changes.

My suggestion for working through this book is to keep it simple and achievable. Start small and work your way up to the bigger concepts. Read the book and choose one or two things that resonate strongly with you and start to action those almost immediately. (You will thank me for this when you see how simple it really is.)

Part I is about making the decision to work with your natural body clock and rhythms, why it's important and why it works. It will help you adopt the mindset required to make this change successful.

Part II shows you what you should be doing and when. It's about how to make the best use of not just your most valuable time, but all your time. It is the heart of this book, packed with lots of tools and techniques to help you be more productive and effective.

After that you can engage with me and other First 2 Hours folks at www.thefirst2hours.com.au or www.facebook.com/thefirst2hours where we share stories, ideas and more tools to help keep you and your team productive and on track.

And throughout this book you will find humour—because work should be enjoyable, not a chore. And reading a book should be a pleasure, not a pain!

So please read, implement, experiment and have fun being more productive!

PART I

WHY THE FIRST 2HOURS?

Many of our productivity problems come about because we are operating on autopilot. We don't think about what, when or even why we are doing things; we just do them in the order in which the tasks came to us, or how they're written on our to-do list.

Just like the default settings of a computer program, our brain also has ingrained settings that it operates with: if I'm hungry, I eat; if I'm afraid, I run. These settings are designed to keep us alive.

Yet some of our less instinctive settings have been developed over years of learning, repetition and reward: in the morning, I check my email; in the afternoon, I hold our department meeting.

It can be very difficult to change settings that feel like they are hardwired. It takes understanding, discipline and practice. But you can do it.

More importantly, there is good reason to do it!

Even though you may be programmed to do things at a certain time because of habit, you are doing yourself a disservice.

When you learn how your body clock works, then you start to understand that there are optimal times for better brain performance at work. This means you can schedule the types of tasks you do to make the best use of your most productive time.

It starts with the first two hours of your day, and continues every two hours after that.

Read on to find out why there are good, better and best times of the day to do particular things, and how you can reprogram yourself to take advantage of that.

CHAPTER 1

Discover what affects your capacity (and your day)

So how do you currently spend the first two hours of your day?

Go on and think about it now.

I bet the first thing you do (like most of us) is open your email and see what pops up. Then, before you know it, it's 1 pm and you're *still* responding to emails or reacting to requests.

NEWSFLASH! You are letting email dictate your day.

Right now, you're wasting your energy and your most productive time on email, instead of on the real work you have to do.

Whether you are conscious of it or not, those emails you have read, replied to or filed create distractions for the rest of the day and make you unproductive. You have given up control of your effectiveness.

Don't worry—this book is not about being anti-email. After all, that's the way most of us communicate at work. What I am saying is that there's a time and a place for everything.

You need to start consciously thinking about the types of tasks you do throughout the day, when you do those tasks and whether you are making the best use of your most valuable time.

Why it's about *when*

There are good scientific reasons as to why we need to pay attention to *when* we do specific things at work.

A lot of this can be explained by jet lag.

When we travel across different time zones, we mess with our body's natural rhythms, known as circadian rhythms.

This is what creates feelings of fatigue and disorientation, and often results in insomnia at 3 am. Shiftworkers, who don't work a typical nine-to-five day, may also experience this quite frequently.

It's when we mess with our body's natural rhythm that we begin to have problems.

That's why we need to do our most important work when our body—and brain—is most awake, alert and ready for action.

For most of us, our most productive time will be first thing in the morning. Then by the afternoon our body and brain will be ready to switch to some routine tasks.

This is best explained by figure 1.1 (overleaf), which is based on the work (likely done in the morning) of Michael Smolensky and Lynne Lambert, published in their book *The Body Clock Guide to Better Health*. It shows a typical circadian rhythm.

As you can see, for the majority of us our peak alertness is at 10 am and our best coordination is at around 2.30 pm.

Tasks that require attention and focus are best done in the morning, and repetitive tasks that require coordination are best done in the afternoon.

So again, let's pause and consider the way you currently work in a typical day.

How does that match up?

If you are like most, you rush through your day from one crisis to another, answering as many emails as you can in the gaps between pointless meetings. It's likely that when you get home from work, you will spend the evening inhaling coffee to stay awake, catching up on correspondence, preparing

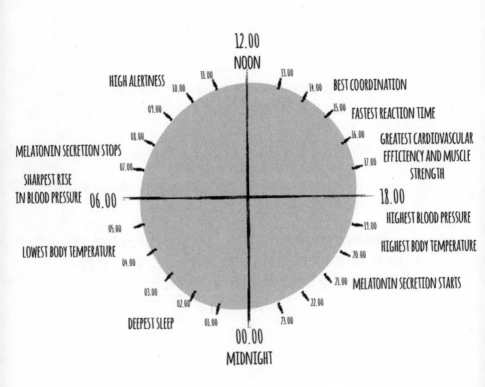

Figure 1.1: typical body clock

Adapted from *The Body Clock Guide to Better Health*
by Michael Smolensky and Lynne Lamberg

presentations for the next day, and getting work done at a time when your body wants to slow down and rest.

You're stuck in a vicious cycle, and it's doing you more harm than good.

Just like what happens with jet lag, if you continue to mess with your natural rhythms you will begin to interrupt your routine sleep habits. This is why it's hard to switch off at night.

We need to pay more attention to the clock in our bodies than the clock on the wall.

I can't decide!

Ever noticed that as the day wears on, your patience (and fuse) in meetings or discussions becomes shorter and more erratic?

If you look at the body clock in figure 1.1, then you'll see why.

At 3 pm when you've been asked to decide between option A or option B—something that could cost the company millions if you're wrong—you've probably sighed and said something like, 'Let's just go with option A and move on.'

When you leave important decisions until the afternoon, then your cognitive alertness is impaired and it's more likely you'll be reactive ('You should be able to make that choice yourself!'), because you're feeling tired from having worked all day.

My friend Sonia says that the one thing that drives her nuts as a working parent is when she gets home from work: the first question she's asked is 'What's for dinner?'

After a day of solving complex problems and negotiating million-dollar deals, she just doesn't have the energy to figure out what everyone is going to eat.

Making important calls, having important discussions and doing important work should be done in the morning before you suffer from 'whatever syndrome', aka decision fatigue.

Just stop and think about this for a minute. For many of us, our jobs require that we make decisions—in fact, it's why we are hired as a leader in the first place! We need good knowledge, experience and the ability to make a sound judgement in our area of expertise.

If you are not making good decisions, then you are putting your career at risk.

Decision fatigue affects everything you stand for, and everything that you, as a manager or leader, are employed for!

One study by Cornell University showed that we make around 200 decisions each day about food alone! Is it any wonder that we are exhausted by the time we have to approve the $1.5-million budget?

This is compounded by the fact that we make decisions every time we open, read and action an email. So, if the email is spam, and the decision we are making is to delete it, that decision uses up options we may need later when we need to formulate a more considered response.

Just think: if we only had 100 decisions available to us before our judgement became impaired, how many of these would we be wasting on email every morning?

When your mental energy is low, depleted by making lots of decisions throughout the day, your brain starts to try and find ways to shortcut thinking. This can result in reckless decisions. Or you might avoid making the decision altogether.

This also explains why some of us lose our temper, make impulse purchases, buy junk food or do something that makes you later think, 'Why on earth did I do that?'

Our self-control wears down, and trying to do too much means we don't end up doing anything well at all. We may even shut down mentally and just accept the status quo.

Both are bad when it comes to work. We don't want our leaders or managers lacking self-control and making reckless or poorly considered decisions, nor do we want people doing nothing!

This is exactly the reason why Barack Obama only wore blue or grey suits while he was the US president — to save his energy for the world's most pressing and important decisions.

Time it right

The evidence shows that our body clock has a natural rhythm and we're often working against it, not with it.

Recent studies show that timing is everything:

» In a 2016 study titled 'Diurnal Variations in Executives' and Analysts' Behavior: Evidence from Conference Calls', researchers found that CEOs who had meetings about earnings with analysts and shareholders were more likely to be upbeat and positive in the mornings. The tone grew more negative as the day progressed. This was an alarming finding, as much of an organisation's value could be determined by how those conversations went.

» The 2011 report 'Temporal Patterns of Happiness and Information in a Global Social Network: Hedonometrics and Twitter' studied Twitter users over a two-year period, finding a pattern that indicated users felt more active, engaged and hopeful in the morning. This plummeted in the middle of the day, and then rose back up again in the early evening. Culture and day of the week had no impact on the findings.

» Another study published in the journal *Emotion* asked over 900 women to choose from a list of adjectives (happy, frustrated, annoyed, enjoying myself, and so on) to characterise how they felt at certain times of the day. The results were almost identical to the Twitter study in the previous point: overwhelmingly, people felt happier in the mornings.

The results are in.

We are happier, more alert, optimistic, considered and energetic during the first few hours of our day, and certainly before midday.

We need to design our day to take advantage of that!

Early bird or night owl?

My friend Rebecca is a 'morning person'. She gets up at 4 am each day. After a coffee and some breakfast, she starts work at 4.30 am and gets her best work done before 7 am. She is usually in bed by 9 pm to accommodate this, but says she can't imagine working any other way.

Another mate, Sharon, gets her best work done between 9 pm and 1 am. She generally goes to bed around 2 am, and, while she gets up around 8 am, she still feels slow until about 9. She needs a lot of coffee in the morning to get going and doesn't feel like she's really at her best until about 1 pm.

Curious about the rest of the people in my world, I posed the following questions on Facebook:

Are you a morning person or an evening person?

What time of day do you feel at your best and most productive?

Of the 76 responses, 67 per cent identified as morning people, and 33 per cent as evening.

The most productive time of day (on average) was 9 am, with most people giving two or three hours of productivity sometime between 5 am and midday.

These results are consistent with most research findings, a lot of which employ the Morning Eveningness Questionnaire, developed by James A Horne and Olov Östberg in 1976. Its main purpose is to measure whether a person's circadian rhythm produces peak alertness in the morning, evening or in between.

Apparently, it is not strictly an either/or question, but rather a spectrum. So some people are more extreme night owls, and some extreme early birds (or 'larks').

While the results vary from study to study, in a normal population:

» between 10 per cent and 21 per cent of people are extreme night owls—surviving on minimal sleep and working late into the early morning

» around 20 per cent are extreme early birds—up, alert and working before many of us have hit the snooze button for the first time

» about 70 per cent are 'normal'—at our most alert between the hours of 9 am and 12 pm.

Statistically then, true night owls are rare.

You may be burning the candle at both ends, which is making you feel tired in the mornings, or you have a job that requires you to work long into the evening (those US conference calls are killers), forcing you to sleep later in the day. Worse yet, you could be messing with your body clock, scrolling through your phone at night.

So if you do your best work at night, then it's worth considering if you're really a night owl or if your schedule or lifestyle is making you one.

Last 2 minutes

We are more alert, cheerful and energetic in the morning, and we suffer with decision fatigue by the end of the day. Hence, we need to think about our work schedule more through the lens of *when* we are doing it, rather than *what* we are doing.

Understanding your circadian rhythm means you can start working with your body and mind rather than pushing yourself against it—that's what Experiment 1 (page 15) will help you with.

Don't fight nature. Work with your body clock, not against it.

A time for everything

In an actual experiment by the Israeli parole board, three prisoners who had completed around two-thirds of their sentences were ordered to appear before the parole board (consisting of a judge, a criminologist and a social worker).

Read the following examples and guess who you think was the most likely to get their freedom, and why.

1. Case 1 (heard at 8.50 am): An Arab Israeli serving a 30-month sentence for fraud.

2. Case 2 (heard at 3.10 pm): A Jewish Israeli serving a 16-month sentence for assault.

3. Case 3 (heard at 4.25 pm): An Arab Israeli serving a 30-month sentence for fraud.

If you guessed Case 1 you would be correct. Despite the fact that the prisoner had the same sentence for the same crime as Case 3, being heard in the morning increased his odds of a favourable decision.

After analysing more than 1000 decisions, it was discovered that prisoners who appeared early in the morning received parole about 70 per cent of the time, while those who appeared late in the day were paroled less than 10 per cent of the time.

This famous study concluded that crime, sentence and ethnic background had little or no bearing on the decision. What had the biggest impact was the time of day that the hearing took place.

EXPERIMENT 1

In his book *When*, Daniel Pink suggests that the simplest way to identify your natural work inclination, or chronotype, is to answer three simple questions:

1. What time do you generally go to bed at night?
2. What time do you generally wake up in the mornings?
3. What is the midpoint between those two times?

For example, if you normally go to bed at 10 pm and wake up at 6 am, your midpoint is 2 am.

Use figure 1.2 (overleaf) to identify your chronotype.

This is of course according to the rule of 'all things being equal'. If you are a shift worker, or if you have recently returned from an overseas trip and your body clock is a bit out of whack, then the results may not be accurate for you. Instead, you could try the free and anonymous online Circadian Rhythm Type Test (AutoMEQ).

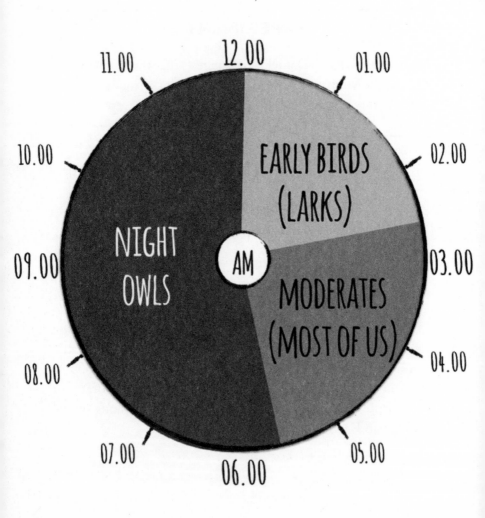

Figure 1.2: your chronotype

Track how you currently spend your time.

» **Keep a list for a week of what you do and when.**

» Start from the moment you wake up, and continue until you go to bed.

» Use table 1.1 to help you. Download the template from www. thefirst2hours.com.au. It's okay to generalise and say 'email' or 'meetings' for a few hours. If you need to, cast your mind back to one or two days last week, and simply capture what you did.

» Analyse the list. What do you find?

» Make some adjustments to what you are doing (it could be as simple as going to bed an hour earlier) to improve your productivity.

Table 1.1: track your time

Time	Activity
7.30 am	Wake up
8.00 am	Gym
9.00 am	Arrive at work—emails for about 1.5 hours

CHAPTER 2
Lay the foundation for productivity

When I ask my clients to tell me about a time when they were at their best, their most productive, they reply with things like:

» after a good night's sleep
» when a deadline is looming
» when I can see tangible results
» working in a great environment
» when it was peaceful and quiet
» with food and water
» following my routine
» being physically active.

Our ability to be productive is influenced by a number of factors (which hopefully you are starting to see), and it is, of course, quite personal. Yet we are all human, which creates some commonalities between us when it comes to our physiology and what we can do to improve how we think and work.

Just like building a house without solid foundations, to-do lists won't work if you lack the energy to complete even the simplest of tasks.

You can try all the time management techniques in the world, but they won't get you far if you are simply not looking after yourself.

The energy to work

Three key factors influence how you work and how well you work—no matter the time of day—as shown in figure 2.1.

Let's look at each in detail.

FUEL

Take a few seconds to cast your mind back over the last few weeks. Can you identify a day where you felt you were super productive? Can you remember what you ate that day?

Think of feeding your body like you're adding logs to a fire. When you put in something like hardwood (complex carbs), then the fire burns for hours before you have to add more. If, on the other hand, you put in a bunch of flimsy paper and cardboard (refined sugars), then you have to keep feeding the fire more and more to keep it going.

Figure 2.1: the three key productivity factors

It's important to think about the fuel or types of food we put into our bodies, because there is a direct ROI (return on ingestion).

What we eat has a direct impact on our cognitive performance.

Our brain needs energy to stay alert and alive. So, if the brain isn't getting enough glucose or energy from the right foods, then we struggle to focus and our productivity takes a dive.

Foods that release glucose quickly, such as bread, cereal or high-sugar soft drinks, give us a burst of energy—but an hour later, we fall into a heap. So, if we are working on hard deadlines, staying glued to our screens and snacking on chocolate bars will tire our brain and body much more quickly than if we took a break to get a healthy lunch.

And guess what else will set in?

Often when we are tired and worn out, we have poor judgement—so hello decision fatigue. It's a vicious cycle: we eat poor food, so we tire and make bad choices. We suffer from decision fatigue so we crave burgers, fries and sweet snacks for a quick hit to keep us going.

A paper from the *British Journal of Health Psychology* says that if we eat more fruit and vegetables throughout the day, not only will we be more productive, but we will also be happier overall.

But *when* you eat is as important as *what* you eat when it comes to energy.

When I eat my homemade granola for breakfast, I work like I am on fire! Like nothing could go wrong!

I travel a lot for work. I bet you do too. I wonder if, like me, you've noticed that hotel breakfasts are both expensive and full of unhealthy (and extremely tempting) choices. So I take my granola on the road. I even make it into breakfast bars so I can get to lunchtime without getting hangry. (I share my recipe for them at www.thefirst2hours.com.au.)

My granola success is no fluke. It's science! Our bodies crave energy when we first wake up. Things such as complex carbs from bread, cereal and fruit, with proteins in the form of milk or yoghurt, are what researchers say is best. (Sadly, no-one advocates Danish pastries first thing.)

The report 'Food Components to Enhance Performance' by the US Institute of Medicine says that having a high-protein, 300-calorie lunch will reduce, but not entirely remove, the effects of the after-lunch slump.

After 5 pm it takes more food to feel full. It's why our dinners are often the largest meal of the day. Our taste buds are more switched on. Our body is also anticipating sleep, so it needs a little fat to keep it going through the night. Again, high-protein meals will leave you feeling fuller than if you have the same number of calories in the form of carbs.

So what can you do to boost your productivity when it comes to fuel?

» *Pack your own lunch*. This way you don't have to make any decisions during the day and healthier options are available to you when you need them.
» *Decide early.* Make the decision about what you are going to eat or snack on before you get hungry—by then it's too late.

» *Graze throughout the day.* Don't wait until you are hungry, then throw in anything you can quickly get hold of from the vending machine.

» *Keep healthy snacks within arm's reach.* Fruit, vegetables, nuts, grains and protein bars are all good, filling options.

In a nutshell, the decision to scoff fast food in ten minutes so we can get back to work will likely have a negative effect on our entire afternoon and evening.

MOVEMENT

A Bristol University study asked 200 employees to assess themselves on a day with exercise and a day without. The results spoke for themselves. On days when people exercised, they found their levels of concentration were higher by 21 per cent and motivation to work was higher by 41 per cent.

Before you start groaning about having to go the gym, the best form of exercise for increased productivity is low impact, such as yoga, dancing or moderate walking.

According to the American College of Sports Medicine, we should be aiming for around 150 minutes per week of activity in ten-minute increments or more.

Exercise not only enhances your productivity, but also your:

» *Happiness.* Regular exercise has been shown to boost serotonin and dopamine, which are the 'feel good' hormones. Who wouldn't feel more productive coming to work feeling good?

» **Health.** Working out boosts the immune system, making you less prone to colds and respiratory infections, says a study published in the *British Journal of Sports Medicine*. Everyone in the office will thank you for that!

» **Strength.** Your muscle strength will improve as well as your endurance to power through the day, no matter what.

» **Concentration.** Exercising helps increase blood flow to the brain, which increases your focus and sharpens your awareness. Ever had a great idea while running for the bus?

» **Motivation.** The pituitary gland is stimulated and releases endorphins, which create those feelings of euphoria that are important for feeling happy and engaged at work. #lovemyjob

» **Memory.** In a study at the University of British Columbia, researchers found that regular aerobic exercise appears to boost the size of the hippocampus, the brain area involved in memory and learning. No more forgetting the name of that lady who works over in finance and sits next to what's-his-name.

» **Resilience.** Regular exercise has been shown to decrease overall levels of tension, improve sleep and boost self-esteem. Hooray!

Looking at our body clock (figure 1.1, page 6), you'll see the optimal time for exercise is between 3 pm and 6 pm.

Your brain and muscles are all warmed up, and you are less inclined to suffer from an injury. It's also the best time to exercise if you want to de-stress from a busy day.

But really, it's about forming a habit that works for you and works around your schedule.

Exercise will boost your productivity, no matter what time of day.

REST

'I'm operating on two hours' sleep right now!' Remember the last time someone said that to you?

Isn't it funny how this is usually presented as some sort of badge of achievement? The trouble is, sleep deprivation impairs our cognitive ability as much as being over the limit with alcohol.

A study by A M Williamson and Anne-Marie Feyer showed that sleep deprivation (going up to 17 hours without sleep) resulted in impairment levels about the same as having a blood alcohol level of 0.05, which in many parts of the country would be the legal limit for fully licenced drivers, and over the limit for provisional licence holders.

We can blame Thomas Edison for our bravado when it comes to operating on little sleep. He thought sleep was a waste of time and did as little of it as possible. Legend has it he created the electric light bulb so that he could extend the number of hours he could work and not be at the mercy of the sun or candlelight.

He was not alone: Nikola Tesla and Leonardo da Vinci were reported to get between two to three hours of sleep in a 24-hour cycle.

Hence, many argue that you can still be successful on minimal amounts of shut-eye. But you know, I also remember when there was a common belief that people drove better after one or two alcoholic drinks, and there was a time when smoking was considered good for your health.

Benjamin Franklin, who was known to say 'early to bed, early to rise, makes a man healthy, wealthy and wise', regularly got six hours' sleep. Barack Obama and Richard Branson also apparently operate on six hours.

And at the other end of the spectrum, Winston Churchill loved to sleep. He credited his success in leading Britain through World War II to the naps he took. He was a seven-hours-a-day kinda guy.

So who got it right?

According to recent studies, the more you sleep, the more productive you are.

David Dinges of the University of Pennsylvania found that anything less than 7.5 hours of sleep per night has an impact on attention, memory, calculations and moods. After only sleeping five hours per night for seven nights, volunteers had trouble with nearly all aspects of 'normal' functioning. *And* it took them two nights of eight hours' sleep to get back to normal again.

In reality, the longer hours we work, the more tired we get, and the more prone we are to error, procrastination or feeling sluggish. Which means we then need to work even more hours to compensate.

As far back as 1893, studies were conducted to see what would happen if we reduced our weekly working hours by 10 per cent, or cut workdays from nine to eight hours. The result? Working more than 40 hours per week created diminishing returns.

The human body requires sleep for survival! It's why we literally go unconscious for up to eight hours in a 24-hour cycle. Evolution has created sleep as the optimal way for our bodies to restore and regenerate before having to be active again for the remaining 16 hours of the day.

While everyone is different and has different sleep needs, for most of us, poor sleep is associated with bad habits such as overconsumption of caffeine or alcohol, overuse of technology, poor diet and lack of exercise.

Need more convincing to get more zzz's?

One study asked 4000 workers to categorise themselves as good sleepers or poor sleepers. The latter group experienced the steepest productivity losses, spending nearly three times as much of their day on time management alone. They were also less motivated and had difficulty focusing, remembering things and making good decisions.

When we get adequate sleep, we can:

» react faster
» judge decisions better
» remember more
» be more creative
» solve problems more easily
» make fewer mistakes
» lower the risk of burnout.

Now that's a case for sleep, don't you agree?

Phone-Free Zone

According to a 2017 Deloitte survey in the UK, 79 per cent of us confess to looking at our phone before going to bed, while 55 per cent say it's the first thing we look at upon waking up.

How do you measure up against this?

Dr Dan Siegel, who is a clinical professor of psychiatry at UCLA School of Medicine, told *Marie Claire* magazine that:

'People are exposing their eyes to this stream of photons that basically tells your brain to stay awake and not go to sleep yet. You're checking your email, you're looking for texts. It tells your brain don't secrete melatonin yet, it's not time for sleep.'

This all continues to mess up our day and our work.

The neurotoxins that build up during the day usually get cleaned when we have a good night's sleep. If not, then this is what makes us feel groggy in the morning, impairs our memory ('Where did I put my keys?') and affects our attention span. Sound familiar?

Several studies show it also increases the risk of diabetes and obesity, so it really is making you sick.

You could wait for natural selection to change our wiring, or you could decide now to work within the time that your body and brain is built for.

Last 2 minutes

Turns out we *are* what we eat. We are the product of our diet, and sleep and exercise. The surprising (and somewhat comforting) thing is that you don't have to change much to set yourself up for a better day of productivity.

A 20-minute walk during lunch, or reducing the number of coffees or caffeinated drinks you consume after midday, will help. But don't forget to turn off your tech at least 30 minutes before you want to fall asleep!

Once we've given our brain the best chance to do what it's designed to do, we have the best shot at improving our productivity. This means we can now make the most of our most valuable time, which is what we explore in chapter 3.

Substitution is easier than abstinence!
Instead of coffee in the afternoons try herbal tea, or (sugar-free) fruit-infused water.
Instead of the lift, take the stairs.

Start the day before

My client Simone loves her sleep. She's a busy working mum who needs to take care of herself so that she can maintain her energy to get through the day—but it wasn't always this way.

She says she used to go to bed around 1 am because she was catching up on work. Then she'd get up around 6 am and get herself and the family organised with breakfast, lunches, and whatever extracurricular activities needed to happen.

She always felt exhausted and never quite on top of things. So instead of talking to her about the first two hours of her day, I started with the last two hours.

I got her to block out one hour every afternoon to think about what she could do that would have an impact on the way she started the following day. Her strategy was to divide her ideas into work-related and home-related categories:

» Work related:
  - review today's and start tomorrow's to-do lists
  - mark the top three things that would have the greatest impact
  - send any quick emails or action tasks that would get tomorrow started on the right foot.

(Continued)

Start the day before *(cont'd)*

» Home related:

    — prepare meals for the next day: breakfast, lunch and dinner (yes, dinner)

    — decide on everyone's outfit (including kids' sports gear and so on)

    — pack bags for tomorrow—have the kids do their own.

After a while, everyone started pitching in and helping each other out, which began to free up Simone's time in the mornings and re-set her usual rhythm.

Over time, Simone became more productive in the mornings, getting through more work during the day, and, slowly, over a few months, her need to work in the evenings disappeared entirely.

EXPERIMENT 2

Are you a good sleeper?

There are a number of apps that can track how well you're going. These are available for just about all smart phones, smart watches or fitness devices. (Yes, I know, it might seem counterintuitive to turning your tech off at night, but they usually work okay with flight mode on so you won't be disturbed by other notifications.)

Do a bit of research to find the right one for you, your lifestyle and your device.

The best ones are those that allow you to enter a few conditions for the day:

- » whether you have exercised
- » what your stress levels are
- » what you have eaten
- » how much water you have drunk
- » how much alcohol you have consumed.

Start to track your patterns and determine the conditions under which you get the best night's sleep. For example, when I did my own analysis, I found that my best quality sleep was on a Monday night, when I had been for a 20-minute walk in the afternoon and consumed a small glass of red wine—yep, go figure!

Change how you view time.

When someone says 'I don't have time for exercise', what they are really saying is 'Exercise is not a priority for me'.

» Think about the reasons why you may not be eating as well as you should, or moving as often as you could, or sleeping as well as you might. What are you putting ahead of your own health?

» Make just one of these things a priority over the next month.

» See what changes. How does your overall productivity and happiness improve?

CHAPTER 3
Design your best day

In 2011, the film *In Time* was released starring Amanda Seyfried and Justin Timberlake. The plot is in the future, with people being engineered to stop ageing on their twenty-fifth birthday. After they turn twenty-five, they have to 'earn' time in order to keep living—they have a clock on their forearm measuring how much time they have left, and when it reaches zero, that person 'times out', or drops dead.

Time is the universal currency in this movie, and can be earned through work, transferred between people or saved onto 'time capsules'. A cup of coffee could cost three minutes, and buying a house could cost you 30 years.

Some people live day to day, while others are immortal, with tens of thousands of years on their clock. Those considered poor are always running to 'save time', while the rich have enough time to meander down the streets, window shopping.

I think about this film a lot, not necessarily because of the acting, script writing or cinematography, but because of this basic premise.

If time were a currency, would you think differently about how or where you spent it?

Would you continue to accept meeting requests and fill your calendar without thinking about how much time you give, to whom and when? Or would you be thoughtful and considered about when you scheduled meetings? (My book *The 25 Minute Meeting* can help with this.)

We need to think differently about how we manage our time, the same way we are encouraged to manage our money or budgets.

If every minute had a dollar value, how would you ensure you got a return every time you gave one out?

Value your time like your property

Traditional approaches to time management involve prioritising, planning, creating to-do lists and ticking off goals. Yet, despite all of this, if I were to ask you, 'How's work?', your response likely would be, 'Busy!'

And along with busy, you would be feeling tired. They usually go hand in hand.

So in many respects we are flipping time management on its head here, and truly thinking about what managing time means, not just how you go about doing it.

When we are truly managing our time, we are thinking about it as a valuable resource that we want to get the best return on. Like money, once time is gone, we are unable to get it back. *And,* unlike money, we can't save it or store it, so we have to make the best use of every minute of the day.

Some people earn very little money and still manage to do a lot with it, and others who earn a lot often don't have much to show for it. It's the same with time, except we all have the same amount of time. And some people seem to be able to achieve a lot more than others.

So answer the following questions honestly:

» Is there a time of day when you feel the most alert and energetic?

» Is there a time of day when you feel foggy and tired?

» Which of these two times, therefore, would you consider the most valuable?

If you consider your alert and energetic time to be twice as valuable as your foggy and tired time, doesn't it stand to reason that you would be more discerning about what and who you give that time to?

Think of your time like real estate from now on. Beachfront properties with a water view are generally of higher value. Apartments in Hong Kong will be valued differently from those in Manila. Even in a game of Monopoly we have properties that cost more and give you a greater return than others.

You need to value your time the way the world values real estate.

Stop multitasking *now*

Seeing as we're talking about valuing our time, I cannot stress how important it is to rid yourself of one terrible habit: multitasking.

Yep, multiple browsers open on our screens, juggling 20 tasks in an effort to get things done faster.

Add to this 'busywork', such as email, tidying the office, updating the filing system, and all those smallish tasks we do when we are procrastinating. This actually creates 'visible progress', which, according to Jason Fox in his book *The Game Changer*, is one of the key motivators for most of us.

With visible progress, I can see the pile of files reducing as I put them away, I can see the space clearing as I tidy the office and I can see the number of emails in my inbox reducing.

When you complete these tasks, it feels *amazing*! Not because you have completed an important or impactful piece of work, but because you got to the bottom of a pile.

When time is a scarce commodity, we go harder and often tick more off the list to get the feeling of satisfaction that comes with that.

But what's the real cost?

According to a *Psychology Today* article, multitasking decreases productivity by up to 40 per cent.

So, by trying to do multiple things at once you are actually *adding* time to the completion of both.

Even worse, multitasking really is an addiction. Our brains are distracted by novelty. This is why we tend to break up our work by checking social media, email, what's on TV.

Our reticular activating system (RAS) is, amongst other things, responsible for helping us figure out where we should focus our attention. Unfortunately, it's also wired to pay attention to newness or novelty, a survival instinct that in the past helped us react quickly to changes in our environment.

When we see something new or different, and we pay attention to it, there is a release of dopamine in our brains. Dopamine generally makes us feel good, and that, in turn, makes us want more.

Like any addiction, over time what once gave us our hit isn't enough. We end up having to do more of the addictive behaviour to get the same pleasurable hit. So, if you are currently checking your email ten times per day, in the future you will have to check it 20 times per day to get the same positive feeling.

Next time you are watching TV, pay attention to how long it takes before you get the urge to check your phone for something. If you are average, it will be around every ten minutes, according to a study by global technology company Asurion.

This has a direct effect on our productivity because it makes us work inefficiently, which takes longer, which means longer hours, which means we are overtired, overworked and overstressed.

**It's a vicious cycle of unproductivity.
Check yourself into multitasking rehab, now!**

Intensity versus impact

By now, you are starting to rethink how you make the best use of your most valuable time by not squandering it on silly tasks or giving it away to the undeserving.

Yet designing your day better still means figuring out what needs to be done that day. However, rather than writing down and working through a long list of tasks, we should run our tasks through the filters of **intensity** and **impact**.

Intensity is the amount of brainpower a task will require. Does it need deep thinking, concentration and focus (high intensity)? Or can you do it with a blindfold on and one hand behind your back (low intensity)?

Another way of thinking about intensity is to use the metaphor created by Daniel Kahneman in his book *Thinking, Fast and Slow*.

In it, he describes the brain as having two systems:

» System 1 is fast, instinctive and emotional. It moves quickly and makes snap judgements. It also doesn't require much energy.

» System 2 is slower, more deliberative, and more logical. It takes deeper thinking and uses a lot of energy. Often, we feel tired or 'brain dead' if we have been using System 2 a lot.

Kahneman also found that the brain tries hard to be frugal with energy. When it detects a moment where System 2 might be about to be engaged, it wants to get System 1 to take over.

Food, exercise and sleep are all physiological elements that can have an impact on your ability to do work that requires intensity, as explored in chapter 2.

We need to schedule work that requires intensity for when we are at our most alert and energetic.

Impact is the return you will get on the time and energy you spend.

If a task will have a high impact or return, it should be prioritised more highly than something that has low impact. To be clear, your first priority will be the impact on you and your personal work, then impact on the team, and then impact on the organisation.

If we can get all three, then it's a natural winner—however, sometimes we can end up spending a lot of time doing things that are of low importance to us or have little impact on our progress.

It might surprise you to learn that, for most of us, there are just two or three things that we need to do in a day that will have the biggest impact on our productivity and results.

The Pareto Principle, for example, explains that 20 per cent of our activity will give us 80 per cent of our results. This concept originated from Italian economist Vilfredo Pareto when he noticed that 80 per cent of the country's land was owned by just 20 per cent of the population. This led Pareto to examine this imbalance further and how it related to other areas, including how we spend our time, effort and energy.

There are hundreds of things that will happen throughout the day, but it's only two or three high-impact tasks that we need to spend our most valuable time on.

WHICH TASKS WHEN?

When it comes to scheduling tasks, we need to think about how much energy, or intensity, will be required so that we choose times when our alertness is at its best.

We can plot our tasks on figure 3.1, to help us visualise and think about the work we need to do first in the day.

1. *High intensity/high impact.* Tasks that directly and positively affect your work and results and require a lot of attention, energy and focus. This is your most important work. If you ever find yourself saying, 'I need to book a meeting room or work from home so I can concentrate on this', then this would be an example of a task that falls into this category. (We explore this further in chapter 4.)

2. *High intensity/low impact.* Tasks that require you to be on your game, and may be in the service of others. Ever had someone ask if they could pick your brain on something? Or bounce an idea off you? That is high intensity/low impact. (Chapter 5 helps you manage this.)

3. *Low intensity/low impact.* Tasks that you can almost do in your sleep because they are easy and the stakes are low. Time often flies when we are here because we are on autopilot doing things that are repetitive and routine in nature. (We discover more about this in chapter 6.)

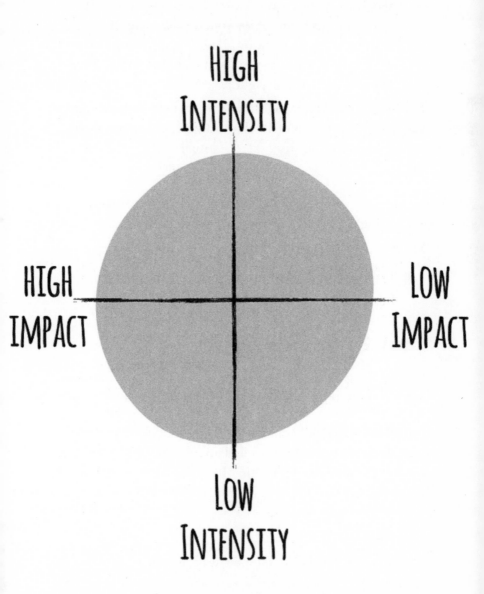

Figure 3.1: intensity versus impact

4. *Low intensity/high impact.* Tasks that don't require a lot of 'heavy lifting' brain-wise, but will have a positive impact on your world: planning, maintenance, preparation. Basically, anything that will set you up for a successful next day. (In chapter 7 we learn to end the day right.)

If you design your day like this, when someone asks you, 'How's work?', you'll be able to answer either 'productive' or 'unproductive' instead of the usual 'busy', 'frantic' or 'stressful'.

I'm sure you have heard the old adage of doing the same things and hoping for a different result. If you want to improve the way you work, you will need to make some changes.

It'll require you to change your habits, but it will have a greater impact on your productivity.

Last 2 minutes

It's time to hit the pause button and ask yourself the question, 'Am I making the best use of my most valuable time?'

Too often we squander our time multitasking or on busywork, or we're driven by the urgency and importance of other people. We rarely stop to think, 'Is this what I should be working on? Is now the right time for me to be working on that?'

Well, no more!

In part II, we determine the best way to plan your workday and your tasks by time, so that you get the greatest return on energy spent.

TIMING TIP

Take a leaf out of Scrooge's book. Be miserly, or at least frugal, with where you spend your time.

Create your own purple patch

I had a client, Li, who was struggling to value his time. He felt like he never had a chance to get *his* work done. He was always in meetings, responding to hundreds of emails per day and then working late into the evening, missing out on time with his family.

From time to time, he would fluke into what he called 'purple patches' where he was able to be super productive. Generally, it was when a meeting had been cancelled and he suddenly had a space in his diary where he could do some, in his words, 'actual work'.

We decided together that he needed to create 'purple patches' more consciously in his diary and I suggested that he block out the first two hours of every day. He then colour-coded this blocked time with the colour purple.

Within three months, he was regularly having 'purple patches' and getting on top of things.

Occasionally he had to be flexible and allow some of his purple time to be shared with others, but for the most part he was able to keep it clear in his diary.

EXPERIMENT 3

What excuses are you making right now that prevent you from valuing your time?

Do you say things like:

» 'I have to do email first thing otherwise I don't feel under control.'

» 'I'm great at multitasking. I get more done when I do several things at once.'

» 'I pride myself on being available at all times for my team.'

Change now!

Don't think of this as a chore, but rather make it a bit of a game or challenge.

For example:

» 'How many days in a row can I avoid opening my email until 12?'

» 'How many tasks in a row can I do without multitasking?'

» 'How long can I go without being distracted?'

» 'What's my personal best (PB) for the number of unimportant emails I can file or delete in a 25-minute burst?'

Just try it and see.

Stop multitasking.

»   Work in short, focused stints. Try the Pomodoro Method, developed by Francesco Cirillo, which advocates focused work for 25 minutes followed by a five-minute break. It's my go-to method and how I wrote this book.

»   Remove distractions. Clear the desk, put the phone on silent and in a drawer, and put your headphones in to deter passers-by. (Studies have shown that noise has a major impact on productivity, and that silence is better than music.)

»   Complete one thing at a time. Finish one job before you start the next. Close the loop.

»   Say 'no' to more tasks. Period. Know thy limits.

PART II

HOW TO MAKE THE MOST OF YOUR FIRST 2 HOURS

Now that you know why you need to design your day better, you can take back control. Not just of your calendar and email, but your whole life!

By identifying the tasks that require the most energy or intensity from you, and those things that also get you a great return on your investment, you can schedule your day according to the best time to do that work.

Most of us work an average of eight hours per day (or at least would like to!) so that's what we're aiming for here.

We're going to carve up our day into four two-hour sessions (figure B):

1. First 2 hours: Proactive
2. Second 2 hours: Reactive
3. Third 2 hours: Active
4. Fourth 2 hours: Preactive.

Let's look at the tasks involved in each of those sessions that will help you maximise your productivity and get the most out of your day.

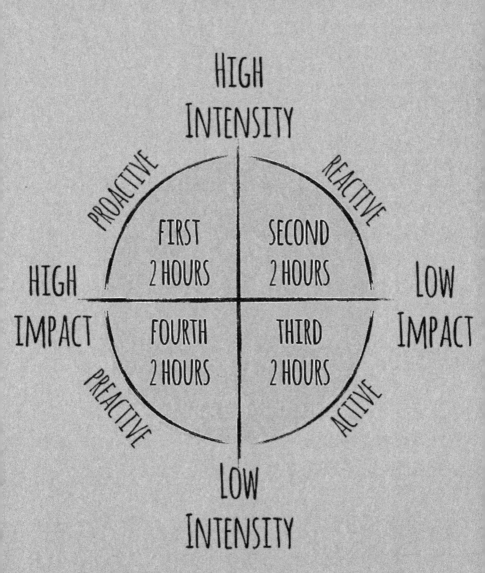

Figure B: your day

CHAPTER 4
First 2 hours Proactive

Too often I hear people complain that they spend their whole day in pointless back-to-back meetings, or running from one crisis to another and never getting what they consider to be their 'real' or important work done.

Scheduling **high-intensity** and **high-impact** work for the first two hours is the first step to truly managing your time.

Not only are the first two hours likely to be our optimal time for getting stuff done, it's also the time where we can set ourselves up for success. The first two hours are good for the tasks listed in figure 4.1 (overleaf).

Getting the right things done first means the rest of the day will almost sort itself out.

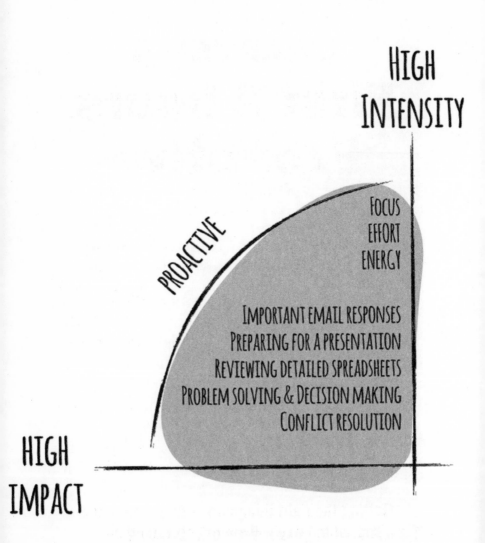

Figure 4.1: your first 2 hours

Choose wisely

It's the time of the day when we can be *proactive* by choosing what we need to do and taking control. It's the time for you to work on the things that will give you the greatest return on your energy-input investment.

The first two hours is when we have the greatest levels of alertness and mental capacity, so we need to make the most of it on the most difficult jobs or the things that require great attention.

Protect this time vigorously! Block it in your diary so you have greater control as to how it is used.

There are three things (shown in figure 4.2, overleaf) we leverage when planning our work for the first two hours:

1. *Focus.* Our concentration is high, especially when we remove distractions to successfully complete difficult tasks. Keep your head down, free from distractions, and concentrate.
2. *Effort.* We are more willing to do harder work, so identify those things that may need extra effort. Put in the hard yards to get the tough jobs done.
3. *Energy.* We know we have the power to complete the tasks that may drain our brain battery later. Use your energy and brainpower to its best effect.

Tasks for your first 2 hours

What we do in our first two hours will always vary from job to job and the demands of our work. As long as you consciously

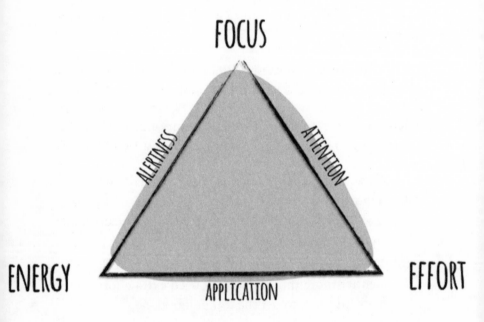

Figure 4.2: resources for the first 2 hours

make the decision that what you are doing requires intensity and is impactful, you will be good.

Ask yourself:

» Does it require deep concentration and focus?

» Is extra effort required to get it done?

» Would it be harder to do, or would there be more risk of mistakes, if I were to do it when I was tired?

» Will this have a high impact on my productivity and performance?

For example, if you are a book editor (like the one who edited mine), then reading, reviewing and editing is going to be your most important work, to be done in the morning. Things such as collating sources or references, formatting fonts and doing the layout might be better for later in the day.

As a trainer and facilitator, I'm front of room most days. However, on office days, my first two hours is spent designing sessions, writing workbooks, putting proposals or quotes together, or developing new content.

If you are a manager in a corporate environment, then this is the time when you should be doing the following tasks.

PREPARING FOR AN IMPORTANT UPCOMING MEETING

I used to think people were demonstrating agility by going from one meeting to another. Now I realise that, although you can go from one meeting to the next, the quality of those meetings is pretty poor. If you have an important meeting coming up, you need to set time aside to think about and prepare for it.

Spend this time preparing a solid agenda that you send out well in advance, or making sure the numbers on the report are accurate *before* you present to everyone else and realise there's a stuff-up!

PUTTING SLIDE DECKS TOGETHER FOR AN IMPORTANT PRESENTATION

While I'm not a fan of PowerPoint, many organisations consider it a fundamental part of how we communicate ideas during meetings.

Unfortunately, most slide decks are put together poorly and with little thought to the audience. If it is an important meeting, and you are trying to influence or sell, you need to make time to put that deck together consciously and thoughtfully, thinking about your outcome and your audience's needs.

COMING UP WITH A PROJECT PLAN

I can't tell you how many times managers say to me that they don't have time to properly plan out a project. Then they'll add that because of hectic schedules and back-to-back meetings, they end up doing it on their own time.

This is exactly the type of task that requires attention and focus to do well. It's not a last-minute, rushed-together-when-the-kids-are-in-bed kind of job. Think of the impact this will have on the project overall.

SOLVING PROBLEMS OR RESOLVING CONFLICT WITH OTHERS

When we are tired and stressed, we are generating more cortisol in our systems, which makes the 'fear' parts of our brain interpret conflict situations as a threat, cutting us off from our executive functions. If there is a problem or issue with others, you need to have all your resources available to you so you can concentrate and make good comments or contributions. Schedule dealing with them in the morning when you are in the best shape.

MAKING IMPORTANT DECISIONS

Remember, we only have a limited amount of decisions available to us in one day, so we want to make sure we are not using them all up in the morning for inconsequential things (what I'm wearing, what I'm eating, and pointless emails).

What else needs a considered response from you?

EXECUTING CONSIDERED AND THOUGHTFUL REPLIES TO EMAILS

The only emails you should be doing first thing in the morning are those that require your attention and need thinking time. More often than not, when we are replying to emails when we are tired or stressed, we make mistakes. They can be as small as misspelling a client's name or as big as blowing up a deal because of some ill-considered wording.

This is such an important topic that we are going to dig deeper into this now ...

The first 2 hour rule:
Action the tasks that require the most brainpower.

Learning to leverage email

Unfortunately, most of us start our first two hours wasting our most productive time on bad habits. We come to work, grab a coffee, chat with a few colleagues, sit at our desk, and then immediately open our email and generally respond to them from the top down. We allow the time at which the email arrived to determine whether we should read it or not.

Do not waste your first two hours on email.

According to an article by DMR, a company that looks at social media statistics and trends, the average user gets around 112 emails per day. I've asked many groups over the past few years this very question, and it varies from 40 to 200 per day depending on the role.

Then I ask, 'What percentage of those are important and require a considered response from you?' The answer was almost unanimously 10 per cent (although a study by the University of Glasgow found that we use email correctly to leverage time zones or answer a well-defined question only 20 per cent of the time). The rest is a waste, and much of it could have been better handled by a phone call or face-to-face discussion.

While I am not telling you to abandon email entirely, I am saying you need to have a system in place to manage it at the right time.

HOW TO SCAN YOUR EMAIL

In his book *Smart Work*, Dermot Crowley has some great advice for handling email. He explains there are three types of email:

1. Action
2. Information
3. Junk.

In the first two hours of your day, you should only be handling the Action emails: those that require some kind of response or action from you. Information and Junk should be cast aside to be reviewed at a low-intensity time of day.

So the new habit I want you to get into is to *scan* your email first thing in the morning and make some conscious decisions about what requires action, and when. For the most part, you will be handling the bulk of your email later in the day. Follow these five steps:

1. Run down the inbox and identify the 10 per cent that require a considered response. (Colour-code senders so you can quickly identify those from your boss!)
2. Determine if those responses are needed immediately or can be scheduled.
3. If it's not urgent, and it requires a considered response, then schedule it for the first two hours tomorrow, or another morning later in the week.
4. Leave the rest until later in the day (more on that in chapter 5).

5. Get rid of stuff that has already been handled or is old. This is another task to leave until later in the day. One of the biggest factors in creating overwhelm at work is seeing the number of emails in your inbox, irrespective of whether you have read them or not. These days the search capability in email is very good. My suggestion is that you only need one additional folder in your inbox, titled 'Done'. Once an email has been read or actioned, you can drag it across. If you need it in the future, provided you remember whom it was from and a rough idea of the subject line and date, you will be able to find it.

> **Email is important, and there is a time for it—just not during the first two hours.**

Remember: *proactive, not reactive*

Let's face it: proactively choosing the most important work for you to do is going to require *a lot* of discipline.

Have you ever walked into the office first thing, and immediately been hit with a crisis, or someone else's problems? If you are a good person, your instinct may be to immediately react and respond.

This can be exacerbated by the level of emotion being exhibited by those pulling us in. If the amygdala in our brain engages, then we will also react and get sucked into the drama.

Before we know it, we have given our attention, focus and energy to things that don't necessarily give us the greatest return and we have wasted that high-value time. Not only that, it is exhausting!

It's not always easy to stay calm and dissociated when you are hit with a tsunami of anxiety, but trust me, you will be the voice of reason and calm when you are able to:

» Hit the pause button.

» Ask yourself (and others): What is really going on here?

» Check what else you had planned to do first up and prioritise accordingly.

» Ask: How can we best approach it?

With planning and practice, you can park non-relevant issues for later.

Last 2 minutes

By being aware of our bad habits, and beginning to mitigate them, we are giving ourselves the best opportunity to maximise the first two hours of the day, which are when we are operating at full capacity. Our tanks are topped up and ready for action! This is the time when we are able to think clearly and are at our best.

This is why the first two hours is so crucial — it will literally set you up for every other hour of work you do from this point on.

So now you have your most important things done first, you are free to leverage the best of your second two hours. This is when your intensity is still high, but you can be more flexible and accessible in support of the work of others. Let's explore that next.

Turn off alerts. Not just for the first two hours, but forever. It will help you stay focused.

Make the impossible possible

Dave always checked his email first thing in the morning. His rationale was that overnight, colleagues from all over the world were messaging him with demands that he needed to respond to *immediately*.

When I pointed out that they wouldn't be reading his emails until 4 pm local time at best, he gawked. That just seemed impossible!

So I asked him to form the habit of scanning his emails first, tagging or identifying those that needed focused attention.

He set up a folder and would drag them into that. Unless there was something that was absolutely critical, requiring his immediate response, he would get on with the things he had already scheduled for his first two hours.

He would review email during or after lunch. Then he would defer some to the next morning, deal with the quick and sometimes mundane emails he had, and respond to overseas requests later in the afternoon, when the recipients were just logging on to work.

An unexpected bonus for this was that, when he left the overseas responses until the afternoon when they were online, sometimes a quick phone call or instant message was enough. This began to have a reducing effect on his email overall.

EXPERIMENT 4

Protect Your Time

Start blocking out the first two hours of your day from now on.

If you have to wait a few weeks until you can begin doing this, that's okay.

However, you could also try and move some of your meetings or other tasks to later in the day. Try and reschedule as much as you can to free up that time, and then protect your two most valuable hours.

Control Your Inbox

Start to practise how you control your inbox. Spend no more than five minutes on this in the morning and set a timer on your watch or smart phone to keep you honest.

1. Run down the inbox and identify the 10 per cent that require a considered response.
2. Determine if those responses are needed immediately or can be scheduled.
3. Schedule the responses accordingly (over the first 2 hours of the coming weekdays).
4. Leave the rest until later in the day.

Some additional tips:

» **Unsubscribe immediately from anything you can**, or most of the newsletters that come to that email address. Do it right now. If there are newsletters you like, then set up a rule or folder for them, or follow them on social media instead.

» **Stop sending emails**, so people don't always feel they have to return one to you! Use instant messaging services for quick communication and save email for things that require considered responses, an evidence trail or attachments.

» **Send better quality emails.** Put the action required in the subject line, for example 'Action required', 'FYI only', 'Please respond' or 'Decision required'. Also, put as much in the email as you can to help the other person respond. I once went back and forth for about eight messages just to set up a meeting. If I had done a better job in the first email, I would have only needed two!

Maximise your first 2 hours.

» Block time out for your first two hours in your diary every day.

» Plan what you will be doing during this time.

» Remove opportunities to be distracted:
  — close the door in your office if you have one
  — work from home
  — move to a quiet room or different location
  — turn off alerts on phones and your computer.

» Consider very carefully any requests to use this time outside of your plan.

» Develop some rituals that support you:
  — come in ten minutes earlier to grab a coffee or tea
  — identify your top three tasks for each day
  — spend the first ten minutes of your first two hours scanning, reviewing and planning.

CHAPTER 5
Second 2 hours Reactive

Imagine you are in a ballroom, dancing. Most of your concentration is on your partner and dancing without stepping on their toes, or the toes of other nearby couples. You tend to be focused on the task at hand.

However, if you were to go up onto the balcony, you would find yourself with a view of the whole room, being able to observe patterns of movement, locate certain people, identify chairs, bathrooms, bars and food tables. You get a bigger picture.

You might recognise this as a concept introduced by Ron Heifetz in his book *Leadership without Easy Answers*. I want you to apply this thinking here.

If the first two hours is about being on the dance floor with your head down and getting impactful work done, the second two hours is about getting up onto the balcony to see what else is going on.

It is about identifying where you need to put your attention now that the most important things are under control. The second two hours are good for the tasks listed in figure 5.1.

The second two hours are about reacting to others' needs now that you have spent time working on what is most important to you.

Attending to others' needs

While the first two hours is about being proactive—getting a head start on the most impactful things—the second two hours gives you the space to be reactive and respond to your urgent needs, or those of your team or organisation.

This is when you have space in your diary for other people to book your time: when your energy and attention is still up and positive, and you're able to respond to their requests.

The tasks you're responding to might be high-impact for them (and possibly you too), but are not as high on your priority list.

The good news is that it's still prime time in terms of your thinking; you've got a couple of hours to go before it's time to break for lunch.

The second two hours (figure 5.2, overleaf) is all about:

- » *Flexibility.* Protecting time where I can react to what needs to be done.
- » *Accessibility.* Giving time and space to people who might need me.
- » *Support.* Where I work on things that may not be high impact for me personally, but are high impact for others.

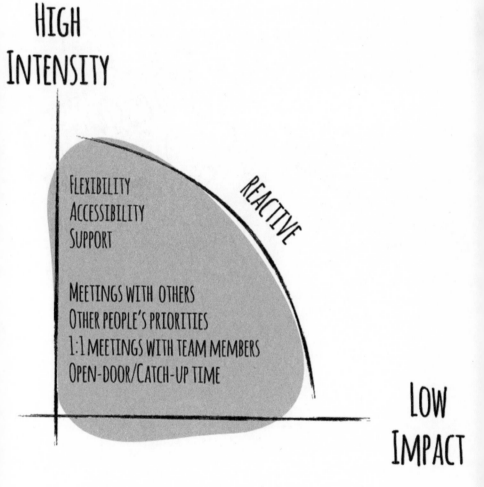

HIGH
INTENSITY

FLEXIBILITY
ACCESSIBILITY
SUPPORT

MEETINGS WITH OTHERS
OTHER PEOPLE'S PRIORITIES
1:1 MEETINGS WITH TEAM MEMBERS
OPEN-DOOR/CATCH-UP TIME

REACTIVE

LOW
IMPACT

Figure 5.1: your second 2 hours

Figure 5.2: resources for the second 2 hours

A spontaneous plan

Some might say that what you are doing in the second two hours is what a normal workday looks like for them: attending meetings, solving problems, dealing with urgent matters, putting out spot fires.

However, working at that pace all day, every day, leads to stress, exhaustion and, eventually, burnout.

It would also be foolish to think that everything at work could be planned and dealt with in a calm, methodical way. There will always be crises that happen, or urgent problems that need to be solved. Yet the more we take care of in the first two hours, the more opportunity we have to be flexible in the next two.

At the end of the day, we can't just make stuff like this go away altogether. The reality is that sometimes, sh*t happens!

But we can learn to choose to be reactive or not.

Your intensity at this time is still high and your alertness is good. So your ability to process information and be creative is now available for others.

One of my colleagues gets into the office at 7.30 am and spends the first two hours doing her high-intensity, high-impact work. Then she opens herself up until lunchtime to accept meetings, do other things for people and generally be available for her team.

Her team has come to know this routine and know that to get the best from their manager, they 'leave her be' until 9.30-ish, when they know they can access her for whatever they need.

It seems counterintuitive to plan your spontaneity, but in the second two hours that's exactly what you are doing.

What should you be doing?

That is the million-dollar question, isn't it? Here are some of the most appropriate tasks for this time of day.

OPEN-DOOR TIME OR CATCH-UPS

In a 2016 article in *Forbes*, it was suggested that the most productive managers are those that have closed-door time and open-door time. This is opposed to the permanent-open-door management theory that was popular in the 1980s and 1990s.

The first two hours of your day is definitely your closed-door time. You are discouraging distraction, increasing focus, or having meetings that require your undivided attention. The second two hours is when you should schedule your open-door time.

It might seem odd to schedule time to be flexible, but if you have a high walk-up rate, then that's why scheduling it works. Letting people know the time they can come in and contact you will be far better than them just 'dropping by' at all times of the day.

Some people use the third two hours (otherwise known as the after-lunch slump) for their open-door time—and if that works, then keep doing it. My caution if you are setting up a routine from scratch, though, is that often you need to be on your game mentally to be reactive to the needs of others. Therefore, the second two hours might be the better time for this.

ONE-ON-ONE MEETINGS WITH TEAM MEMBERS

While there is a positive impact on your work when you meet with your team members regularly, the more you schedule them at certain times, the less likely you are to have unexpected interruptions at other times.

Regular formal, or spontaneous informal, coaching and/or mentoring of others is also perfect at this time, as you are more able to give their needs your full attention.

Most people seem to think there's a magic number when it comes to regular meetings with team members, but I think it depends on a number of factors, such as the experience of the team members, the nature of their work, the level of input required by the manager and the number of team members they manage. Agreeing on a mutually appropriate cadence, reviewing after 90 days and adjusting if required is a good approach.

What is more important is that, whatever frequency you agree to, you are consistent. One of the worst things a manager can do is schedule regular one-on-one meetings and then cancel them when other priorities get in the way. Your availability and commitment to these types of meetings sends a clear message about how much you value your team members.

In return, they will value your time (at the right time).

CARRY-OVERS FROM THE FIRST 2 HOURS

Don't feel rushed or pressed to down tools and change all your tasks if you're still bright, alert and continuing on high-impact work from the first two hours. If there is something that requires more time, then go ahead and block out four hours.

Just be aware of unconsciously blending the first two and second two hours. It's really easy, when your head is down and you are getting important stuff done, to stay there and keep working.

At the very least, stop after the first two hours and assess where you're at (get up on the balcony) and see if there is anything needed from others. If not, you can then go back to what you were doing.

HELPING OUT

There are so many things that happen throughout a day that we can't plan for. By having some time set aside in your day, you have more flexibility to cope with all the general things people may need your help with.

These could be things that have emerged overnight or in the very recent past. They may directly affect your high-impact work, or not. It may mean attending a meeting or contributing to situations where your know-how is needed to move a project forward.

Someone asks you to step in and take over part of a project, or develop a slide deck or write a paper. If there isn't time to schedule it for the next two hours, you could do it here.

You may also help others overcome obstacles. Often people will have a problem and it holds up their work until they get a chance to ask someone or get some guidance. Making yourself available for this means projects and work can maintain momentum.

It may be as simple as people needing to bounce ideas off you. Sometimes a team member or colleague may want to talk through an idea, an opportunity or a problem and get your input.

QUICK EMAIL SCAN

If you are doing this right, then it's likely been two hours since you checked your inbox. Run your eye over your email to see if there is anything that requires your immediate attention and you can resolve quickly with a few minutes of considered responses.

But don't go down the rabbit hole! This is still *not* the time to get stuck in and react or respond to your inbox.

To meet or not to meet?

Most of the tasks I've mentioned could be categorised as meetings. The second two hours is often characterised by them because you're attending to the needs of others.

It's important to understand who you are meeting with and why, and being discerning with that time.

You should still wisely choose who you allow into your diary, as this will obviously have an impact on your day.

It's easy to just open up the diary and let people fill that time, clicking 'Accept' for every invite that comes in.

So to help disrupt this habit, you could try some of the following:

» *Draw a line in the sand.* Go as far ahead in your diary as needed to start blocking time for yourself. Depending on how busy your calendar is, you may have to go several weeks into the future. Then, be selective and disciplined when giving this time away to others.

» *Break meeting time into four 30-minute increments.* First come, first served. Give them time in your schedule to lock this in. This allows you to spread the love around rather than being focused completely on one person, problem or situation for the whole of the two hours.

» *Set limits.* Decide how much time you will allow for meetings, and how long they will be. Science says 25 minutes is best. I dig into this in my book *The 25 Minute Meeting*, and, in a nutshell, 25 minutes allows you to keep it short, sharp and focused. It also gives you a five-minute break between meetings to gather your thoughts and prepare for the next. Be careful, though: if your second two hours is constantly 'booked out' with back-to-back meetings, then you are hardly being accessible and spontaneous!

Above all else, remember to meet wisely and with people and projects that truly need your attention.

Last 2 minutes

The second two hours is designed for you to be open to and supportive of the needs of others. This is about helping your team, colleagues and co-workers with their high-impact projects. Just don't become a slave to meetings!

Make yourself available to deal with urgent, proximate and pressing issues for yourself and others, but you must take a break and enjoy lunch before diving into the tasks of your third two hours.

Remember from chapter 2 that you are what you eat. Creating a foundation for productivity in the afternoon comes directly from what you consume at lunch. Whatever it is, it will set you up for the next part of your day.

TIMING TIP

Decide how many meetings you will accept per day or week, and, once you have hit that limit, consider yourself 'booked out'.

Get 'in the pit'

Ivan was in the privileged position of having his own office. This meant he could schedule open- and closed-door time quite easily.

However, he found that, even when his door was open, people weren't coming in.

At first, he took advantage of that and extended his first two hours to the next two. Yet he started to feel isolated from his team, and his scheduled one-on-one meetings were a bit stiff. He believed there were a few reasons for this.

His highly hierarchical organisation meant that people were sometimes nervous about 'bothering' senior people, and his office was not conducive to being relaxed. It had a very formal layout and required him to sit opposite his visitor at a massive table.

So he decided to do his second two hours from a desk out with the team.

At first, they were a bit taken aback and still avoided speaking to him. But then a pattern formed, and a few people started coming to him more casually. He found that the team opened up and made good use of his time 'in the pit', as they referred to it.

From time to time he would take people into the office if they needed a private conversation, but for the most part he enjoyed the couple of hours a day he would spend out with the team.

EXPERIMENT 5

Make sure you are reacting to the right things.

How often do we have the assumption of urgency? We use words like 'soon', 'quickly' or 'by Friday' without really understanding what that timing means. Even the phrase 'we have plenty of time' means different things to different people.

People set arbitrary deadlines like 'close of business' when it actually could be delivered at 10 am the next morning. 'Close of business' is a mental time stamp that lets people feel like the day is closed off and completed, like a full stop to the day.

Remember, if it's 3 pm and someone says, 'I need you to do this urgently', you may not be in the best frame of mind to get it finished. Making a start and reviewing it in the morning might be a more accurate and productive way of dealing with the work.

Over the next couple of weeks, test your 'urgency' assumptions by:

» asking people for a specific time they want something by. Don't accept 'ASAP', as that can be just as meaningless as 'soon'.

(Continued)

EXPERIMENT 5 *(cont'd)*

» asking people for context around what will happen with the work afterwards—for example, 'Who is waiting on this?' or 'How will what I'm doing affect the work of others, or the project overall?'

» responding, if they say 'I need it by close of business today', by asking 'What would happen if I wasn't able to meet that deadline?' or 'What would happen if I gave it to you by 10 am tomorrow?'

Maximise your second 2 hours.

» Let people know when you are available (or not).

» Be open and flexible with how you spend this time—don't let too many recurring or regular meetings happen at this time.

» Create opportunities to be approached.
  - Open the door to your office if you have one.
  - Move to a different place to work (for example, out with the team, or into a shared or co-working space).
  - Make yourself available on instant messenger and any other internal communications tools.

» Be discerning about how many meetings you fill this time with.

» Develop some rituals that support you:
  - Take a break and get a cuppa to mark the time between the first and second two hours.
  - Take a five-minute stroll around the office and let your team 'see' your availability.
  - Take a minute to scan your emails.

CHAPTER 6
Third 2 hours Active

Unless your workplace encourages siestas, then this time of day, after lunch, is at risk of being a complete waste. Despite the fact that we say it's for our low-intensity and low-impact work, it's still time for work, not milling around the office cooler.

While you could argue that this time of day is the *least* valuable, it is still time that we need to make the best use of.

Sometimes the lethargy of this time of day is hypnotic. Before you know it, you've lost time fiddling around, trying to write an email, or reading the same stuff over and over again before realising nothing is of value. That's why it's super important to get smart about what this time is best used for. Figure 6.1 (overleaf) lists some of the best tasks for this time of day.

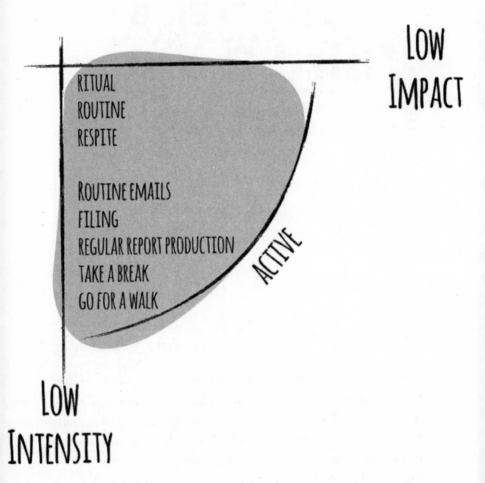

Figure 6.1: your third 2 hours

Just as we should be purposeful about maximising our most valuable time, we can also leverage what could be described as our least valuable time.

Leverage, don't lose it

Now is a great time to do the things you've been putting off for ages! Our attention is low, but our ability to repeat tasks is high, so think filing, organising or anything that you'd consider 'boring'. This is the time of day that is *perfect* for this.

Just because things are routine or mundane doesn't make them unimportant!

Call it your 'quiet time' or 'down time' if you will. Give your brain a break. Work on low-impact activities that require low energy or intensity instead of turning to coffee or sugary soft drinks to get you over the line.

Instead of being at the mercy of this time, let's leverage it!

This is the time when we need to make the best use of the things in figure 6.2 (overleaf):

» **Ritual.** Doing things that are habitual, meaningful and purposeful. Maybe going for a daily walk or having a ten-minute catch-up with a colleague.

» **Routine.** Scheduling work that is 'business as usual' or repetitive and doesn't require too much thinking. These could be regular meetings, or reports you produce on a daily or weekly basis.

» **Respite.** Give yourself a break! If we are working with our natural rhythms and taking some time out we can be ready for the afternoon pick up.

Figure 6.2: resources for the third 2 hours

Yes, wait until late!

At this time of the day, your body is naturally looking for a rest while it digests your lunch. Doing work in short bursts and taking breaks is particularly useful here.

At this time we often experience a drop in attention, memory, logical reasoning and mood. This is not a good time to have a meeting where critical decision making or problem solving is required!

But it is a good time to do things like ... yes ... email!

Finally, this is when you can do your email!

Yes, I know, I know. It does seem ridiculously late to check your email, but hopefully by now, you understand why.

Remember that only about 10 per cent of your email actually requires a considered response, so now you can manage and process the remaining 90 per cent that doesn't require your brain to be at capacity. And ... given that 80 per cent of your emails are probably a waste of your time anyway, there's not much at stake here.

However, I know I can give you all the facts and stats and research you like, and you will *still* find a reason or excuse to not wait until after lunch to answer your emails.

Here's why:

» *'FOMO' (fear of missing out).* The very idea of not checking your emails until after lunch is scary! 'What if there is something important there that I need to respond to?'

» *'All my work comes from email.'* If most of your tasks or direction come from your inbox, how will you know what to do with your day?

Both of these are actually true for most people. We are worried we will miss something important, and much of our work does come via email. The point is that your email inbox is no different from the old-fashioned in-tray on your desk: it's the way that work comes to you. But we need to be more mindful of *when* we process it, respond to it and complete it.

You are learning how to start a new habit of doing most of your email after lunch.

The real trick is to, over time, reduce altogether the amount of email you are sending and receiving. Recent research suggests that email is bad for your health. A UK study showed increased heart rate and blood pressure when government employees were actively using their emails. Not good!

Here are two things you could do right now to reduce the amount of email you receive:

1. *Send less.* Use other communication methods such as phone calls, personal visits or instant messenger.
2. *Improve the quality.* Use the subject line more effectively to indicate the action required, and give as much info as possible to reduce the amount of back and forth. For example, rather than say 'When can we meet', you could say 'Can we meet on Thursday at 2 or Friday at 4?'

As we've explored, this is about shifting your usual patterns and cycle of habits.

People learn how you respond. If you are someone who responds immediately to all emails, then people come to expect that. Then, if you don't reply to something within 30 minutes, you'll get another email or a phone call wanting to know why you haven't responded to the email!

I am a professional trainer and facilitator who can sometimes be front of room for days, and, because I believe in being fully present, I may not look at my emails for a couple of days. I have been working this way for years and most of my clients know and understand this. I have in effect 'trained' them that I will get back to them when I can. They also know that if it is super urgent, they can call or text me, which will get my attention quicker.

Arianna Huffington, CEO of Thrive Global, deletes any messages she receives when on vacation and expects her employees to do so as well. She and her team set up auto-responders that read something like this:

Thank you for your email. I am out of the office until August 27. For anything urgent please email [employee's name and email]. Otherwise, please email me again when I return as this email will be deleted.

What a great way to relax on vacation, knowing you won't be coming back to an overflowing email inbox!

So how have you trained the people who email you?

Luckily, you can also retrain others to expect email responses from you later in the day.

Remember, if the idea of not looking at your emails at all in the morning is too much, then you can SCAN first thing, but don't respond. Use it as a way of assessing how you need to spend the day. (Chapter 4 helps you here.)

If there is something earth-shatteringly, organisation-destroyingly urgent for you to reply to, the SCAN will turn that up.

But the processing of your email—that means deleting, unsubscribing and filing—is done now.

This is the time of day when you can:

» read a newsletter that you have subscribed to
» glance at CC messages and drag them do your 'done' folder
» manage meeting requests (making sure you don't book less impactful meetings during the first two hours)
» respond to emails that don't require a lot of thought
» deal with the FYIs.

Anything that turns up that needs a considered response, we will wait to address in the last two hours of your day. Chapter 7 helps you do that.

Email will likely be the first thing on your mind in the third two hours—but it won't be the last thing you can do.

Rinse and repeat

Other routine and repetitive tasks, which usually feel like groundhog day, can actually be quite pleasurable at this time of the day.

Instead of feeling like you're trying so hard to do something that you just aren't capable of, for example writing that report or editing a document, we can increase our levels of wellbeing, confidence and motivation by doing things that are familiar.

LEARNING AND TRAINING

Studies have shown that when you are learning something new, rates of retention go up if it's done in the afternoon.

So this is a great time to grab that book or article you've been meaning to read and highlight some key notes. Or you might think about teaching others how to do repetitive or routine tasks, such as learning the latest software program or uploading to the intranet.

Err on the side of caution when it comes to PowerPoint presentations, though. Warm, dimly lit rooms are a recipe for naps—no matter what time of day it is.

FILING AND SHREDDING

Despite the feeling of lethargy in the afternoon, some studies have shown that motor skills are better at this time, so if you have physical tasks you could do, then do them. We're talking clearing away that large pile of journals or reading matter, or going through the boxes of files for archiving.

OPERATING ON AUTOPILOT

If the morning is about thinking, the afternoon is about doing.

If the morning is about being strategic, then the afternoon is about being operational.

Operational tasks, such as practising a skill or getting jobs done that don't require a lot of mental processing, are also good to do here.

You might have thought about and planned out a presentation in your first two hours, followed up queries about it with your team in the second, and now, in the third, you could pull together the content for formatting. It's likely to be repetitive in nature as you copy and paste fonts and images throughout the document.

In fact, I find this part of presentation development downright fun! It's the time when I can browse for images, play with the layout and explore my creativity.

CREATING LISTS

At this time of day, our short-term memory function is also at its lowest ebb, so having lists of what you need to do can be helpful. If you have enough routine tasks for this time, create a list so that you can do one each day, and you don't have to remember the tasks you want to perform. Or prepare the list over lunch while you are enjoying your sandwich!

In his book *The Checklist Manifesto*, Atul Gawande cites many examples of checklists that save lives, in situations as varied as flying planes and managing hospitals. We may not need to save lives in our day-to-day work, but checklists are great for:

» ***Doing the basics.*** Checklists help us make sure the minimum gets done. In a world rife with distractions and 'shiny new objects', they keep us focused.

» *Freeing up brain space.* Rather than constraining you, they liberate you so you don't have to remember the regular every time.

» *Creating discipline.* Checklists seem to spur people to get stuff done. It could be the dopamine hit that comes with checking something off.

» *Preventing errors.* They may feel like they are time-consuming to go through, but typically they save us time by preventing do-overs.

Creating lists (as shown in chapter 7) is a great task for the fourth two hours of the day—but the third two hours perfect for applying those lists.

TAKING A BREAK

The biggest issue with this time of day is that you've just come back from lunch, and you're feeling the natural downturn in energy that happens while your body digests food. This makes it a great time to be standing up and moving around.

However, we usually resist taking a break—and this is largely due to those leaders in the world who claim that they can get by on little rest, or see down time as pure laziness. Some wear their sleeplessness as a badge of honour and almost imply that those of us who need some quiet time are somehow less productive. They couldn't be more wrong.

Skipping breaks to make us more productive is a false economy.

A study published in the *Scandinavian Journal of Medicine and Science in Sports* found that people who did a 30-minute walk three times a week during their lunch break were less tense, more enthusiastic and more relaxed.

They also reported that these people could cope with their workload better on days when they walked compared to when they didn't.

Trying to push through for the next few hours without taking a break is likely to make us less productive. If we just walk away for 30 minutes or until we come good again, it's amazing how fresh our eyes feel, and how often we can see the light.

Should you take a nappuccino?

In chapter 1 I discuss my Facebook poll, in which I asked participants about their most productive time of day. My favourite quote from the whole post was '4 am to 6 am. Afternoons are for naps.'

Laugh, like me, if you will, but in China, where I worked for a couple of years, there was one lunchtime habit that was sacrosanct: you had to down tools and sleep after lunch every day. It was a familiar sight to see people put their heads down on their desks for a 30-minute nap.

Could you imagine this in your workplace? What would your boss or colleagues say if you decided to put your head on the table and sleep? Unfortunately, this behaviour is frowned upon and considered lazy in most parts of the Western world (unless you work for Google, which has sleep pods for cat naps). This is a shame, because research shows that an afternoon nap really can boost productivity.

Matthew Walker, neuroscientist and author of *Why We Sleep*, explains that we are in the midst of a 'global sleep-loss epidemic' brought on by demanding work schedules and commutes.

Unfortunately, we tend to turn to coffee to power through. One study showed that a powernap of between 10 and 30 minutes is better than a cup of coffee or can of soft drink. But if you nap more than 30 minutes, you may be at risk of waking up even groggier or, if you nap late in the day, you'll interrupt a good night's sleep.

In *When*, Daniel Pink suggests you have a 'nappuccino': a cup of coffee just before your 20-minute nap (between 1 pm and 3 pm). This is because it takes about 20 minutes for the caffeine to digest and have its effect, so you get a double whammy! You'll feel good from the nap, with an extra boost of caffeine. That last two hours of your day will be turbo charged!

Last 2 minutes

The premise of this book is to work with your body, not against it. If it needs a rest, take it. If it doesn't want to think hard, then do low-intensity work. If it needs to be mobile, then take a walk. The third two hours plays into this perfectly.

Getting some of the more mundane tasks done and out of the way means you now have time to work out what's important before you shut up shop for the day.

You will give yourself a better chance of leveraging the fourth two hours more productively if you take some time out now and give your brain a chance to recuperate after a busy morning.

Use the third two hours to set yourself up for success and productivity for the remainder of the afternoon, because the fourth two hours are when most people get a second wind.

Let's look at that now.

Feeling energised and alert despite the time of day? Take advantage of it and move on to the tasks that belong in the fourth two hours.

No job too low

One of my friends, Mahoba, told me that she waited for the third two hours to get a big pile of scanning and shredding contracts done.

Before she instituted this habit, the pile just kept getting bigger and bigger because (a) it was a low-priority job that no-one wanted to do and (b) no-one really saw it as their job. The bigger issue was that from time to time someone needed to reference a document that was in the pile and it was almost impossible to locate a specific contract without going through each document, one after the other.

Mahoba saw it as an opportunity to keep being productive at a time when she sometimes would glaze over and waste the hour after lunch.

It was a repetitive job that required very little cognitive effort, and it was physical, involving standing up and moving around between the scanner and the shredder.

She scheduled an hour of scanning and shredding after lunch every day and enjoyed all the benefits that came with it. She found it meditative and restful (like napping on her feet) and yet the physical nature of the work had her feeling alert after the hour and ready to take on tasks that require more intensity in the afternoon.

My favourite part about Mahoba's story is that what seemed like a little job, that could have been considered well below her pay rate, contributed to the whole team's productivity. She later told me that after about a week of doing this a couple of people joined her in the afternoons and it became an after-lunch 'ritual' where they would scan, shred and chat for about 30 minutes.

EXPERIMENT 6

How much time could you save if you reduced your email by, say, 20 per cent?

In the example in table 6.1, which is based on the average amount of email my clients tell me they are sending and receiving per day, a 20 per cent reduction could recover 28 days of productive work time.

That's a whole month! What would you do if you had an extra month of time in the year?

Table 6.1: calculate your savings

Actual email received

	Example	You
Number of emails received per day	80	
Multiply by 240 workdays per year (adjust +/–)	240	
Annual email received **A**	**19 200**	

Annual email sent

	Example	You
Number of emails sent per day	60	
Multiply by 240 workdays per year (adjust +/–)	240	

Annual email sent	**B**	**14 400**	

Annual days spent processing email

Add A + B	**33 600**	

× 2 minutes per email	**67 200**	

Convert to hours by dividing by 60 minutes	**1120**	

Divide by 8 work hours per day	**C**	**140**	

Days saved by 20 per cent email reduction

C × 20 per cent	**28**	

Play with the percentage. Start with 10 per cent or go as high as 50 per cent. Play with the math.

Maximise your third 2 hours.

» Make the most of this time to play catch-up.

» Use a timer for really mundane tasks, and do them in short, limited bursts.

» Incentivise your activity. If there is a particularly mundane or boring task, treat yourself at the end with a quick scan of social media, a (healthy) snack, or a chat with a friend or colleague.

» Plan what you will be doing during this time as well as you would for the first two hours. Don't get to the end and realise you have just blown a couple of hours.

» If you are scheduling regular or routine meetings, this is the time to do it.

» Develop some rituals that support you:
   — *Take the stairs.* Go and walk up and down several flights of stairs to get your blood pumping and your body temperature increased. If you can't do that, then just go for a walk.
   — *Hydrate.* Have a big glass of water, at least 500 millilitres.
   — *Snack smart.* Grab a piece of fruit or a handful of nuts instead of sugary or high-carb foods.

CHAPTER 7
Fourth 2 hours Preactive

Finally, you've made it! You're nearing the end of the day.

This is usually the time when people have a heart attack because they realise they've been answering emails all day long and haven't actually got around to any valuable work.

Well, if you've been following the rules, you will find that the last quarter of the day (shown in figure 7.1, overleaf) is all about wrapping up the current day and preparing yourself for the next one. That's why, in many respects, I believe the last two hours of the day are as important as, if not more important than, the first two hours.

It's where you review what you completed today, and set up for tomorrow.

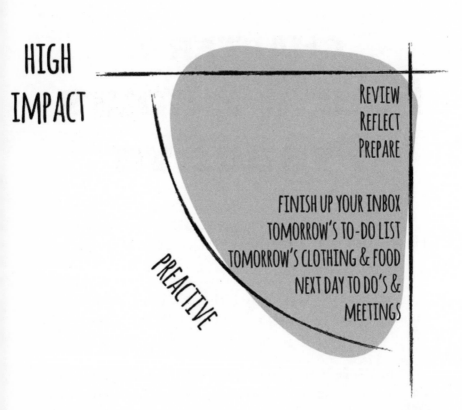

HIGH
IMPACT

PREACTIVE

REVIEW
REFLECT
PREPARE

FINISH UP YOUR INBOX
TOMORROW'S TO-DO LIST
TOMORROW'S CLOTHING & FOOD
NEXT DAY TO DO'S &
MEETINGS

LOW
INTENSITY

Figure 7.1: the fourth 2 hours

Second wind?

Now we are being *preactive*, which means *planning*, not necessarily *doing*, what needs to be done. Things that you do here help reduce the number of decisions you have to make the next day, when you start your first two hours again.

While the specific time varies, many of us experience an upward swing of energy and alertness in the fourth two hours, with a peak around 6 pm. This is often experienced as 'second wind', when we begin to feel a little more energetic and have the capacity to push through. If we're lucky, we end our day with a bang!

During an interview for the *Chicago Tribune*, Timothy Monk, an associate professor at the University of Pittsburgh's Western Psychiatric Institute and Clinic, said that this time of day is best for finishing the day's more important work: to draft key emails, do the expense report and schedule your next day. He also says that, because this is a time when we have a peak in long-term memory, this is a good time to research or read material for a future presentation.

So the focus for this quadrant (figure 7.2, overleaf) is to:

» **Review.** What did I get done (or not) today? What else do I need to do before heading home today? What do I need to make sure gets on the to-do list for tomorrow (scheduled at the right time, of course)?

» **Reflect.** How do I feel about my productivity? Did I make the best use of my most valuable time?

» **Prepare.** How can I best set myself up for success tomorrow?

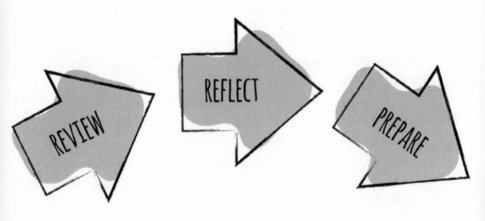

Figure 7.2: resources for the fourth 2 hours

Acknowledge and move on

A friend of mine works for an organisation staffed mostly by engineers. She says they have been trained their whole life to focus on what is broken and how it can be fixed. She says it has created a culture in the organisation where praise and acknowledgement is rare, and criticism and fault-finding the norm.

What many in this organisation don't realise is that this nitpicking, or 'missed a spot' approach, creates a feeling of fear. When people are afraid, they have increased levels of cortisol, which is generally known as the 'stress' hormone. When people feel threatened, for example in a meeting if someone is critiquing their work or asking them to justify their actions or position, cortisol will be released into their system in greater amounts and this makes them stressed out, foggy and forgetful.

You can imagine the impact on team productivity!

The same applies here.

For many of us, we end the day beating ourselves up for all the things we didn't get done and we take this feeling of stress home with us, and to bed, interfering with a good night's sleep.

So let's flip this and take a more appreciative approach.

Let's take a leaf out of my colleague Russell's book. He keeps a journal and scrapbook of things he is proud of accomplishing, and complimentary notes or emails he has received from people. He keeps this so that, on days when he is feeling a bit down or low energy, or wondering why he does what he does, he can get it out and take a look at the positive comments people have made about him and the high-impact projects he has worked on and it gives him an energy boost.

What Russell doesn't realise is that he's giving himself an oxytocin boost! Oxytocin is known as the 'feel-good' hormone and it's great for reducing blood pressure and anxiety, and it stimulates positive social interactions.

If you are a parent, it's what you feel when you first lay eyes on your child. If you're not a parent, it's what you feel when you watch kitten and puppy videos on social media.

You don't need to keep a scrapbook.

Simply having an appreciative approach to work increases our feelings of happiness and wellbeing, which also opens us up to feeling more positive and motivated.

We can stimulate oxytocin production by stopping and asking ourselves what are we proud of achieving today.

So, the fourth two hours is about taking the time to review what you have done and acknowledging to yourself (and, if appropriate, to the team) what you have achieved and the impact it has had.

Obviously, if you didn't achieve what you wanted to achieve, then you need to acknowledge that and plan appropriately for the next day.

Ask yourself:

» Was it a realistic deadline?
» Were there some unexpected things that came up to prevent me from completing the work?
» What could I do differently tomorrow to give me a greater chance of getting stuff done?

In fact, the worst thing you can do is stress out about it, or try and stay back all night trying to get everything done. If you do this, you will worry all night, and wake up the next day already tired and without the ability to do your best work during the first two hours.

Self-edit your movie

If things haven't gone to plan, one of my favourite activities is something called a 'self-edit'. For me I could do a self-edit of a meeting that didn't go the way I would have liked, or a workshop I delivered that fell over in a couple of places, or moments where I wasn't as productive or efficient as I would have liked.

This is actually a high-performance strategy used by many athletes, performers and musicians—anyone who wants to get to or maintain their peak performance.

To perform a self-edit, complete the following steps:

1. Take a moment to run the day through your mind as if it were a movie and, every time something happens that you thought was not the best, hit the pause button and tag it. (Imagine tagging it with a post-it note, or bookmark—whatever works in your mind.)

2. Keep moving through the movie of your day, pausing and tagging as required until you reach the end.

3. Rerun the movie, stopping at each of the tags, and imagine the problem was resolved. Play that part of the movie as if it went *exactly* according to plan. Change the script to be what you wished you had said, what you think they would have said, what you would have done differently, what they would have done differently. Edit the crap out of each of the tagged moments.

4. Run the movie for a third time, with each of the edited pieces now part of the flow. You have completely taped over any of the previous errors or mistakes.

5. Run the film again, if necessary, to cement it in your brain.

The theory behind this is that the mind and body will react the same to actual experiences as it would to imagined or pictured events. It's why you can conjure happy thoughts by thinking about someone you like — it can feel the same as if you actually saw them. This technique is in many ways rewiring the brain to remember the events differently, giving you the opportunity to do things differently in the future.

Tidying up loose ends

Once you have reviewed, reflected and acknowledged what you have done for the day, you may find there are a few loose ends that could be tidied up before packing up and leaving.

Your filter for these should be around time. Will it take you a few minutes to send a few emails, make a quick call, or spell-check a document?

These should be things that will have a great impact on your work, but that don't need too much intensity or brain power. Four o'clock in the afternoon is not the time to start a major project!

If it is going to take longer, or require more attention and energy, then do what you can to give yourself the best opportunity to get it done the next morning.

If you are not careful, you will also end up responding to people's last-minute requests as if you must do them immediately! This is not the case. Your discipline around advising people when you will get stuff to them becomes important here. It's okay to say, 'I'll get that to you tomorrow by noon' as opposed to 'I'll get onto that right now and finish it by tonight'.

There are so many things that should wait until the next morning. In most cases, an email sent at 5.30 pm won't be read until the next morning anyway. So if it's important and there is a lot at stake, save it as a draft, read through it the next morning and then send it when you have more decisions available to you, and your brain is fully recharged.

In fact, a colleague told me that they write their emails at night and then set up their email to send them the next day. This is so the other person doesn't respond to them at night (when they may not be at their cognitive best) and to limit the number of emails sitting in your inbox in the morning.

It also helps to set boundaries, so the other person doesn't think you're a night owl who'll respond to anything and everything at will!

There may also be some other last-minute actions you can take now.

SCAN YOUR LIST AND EMAIL FOR ANY LAST-MINUTE URGENT THINGS

After a couple of weeks of working differently, there should only be a handful of emails that will be coming throughout the day, and you should be able to get to zero inbox before you head home. What we are trying to avoid is having something hanging over your head that might create restlessness and poor sleep.

But it's okay to do a quick scan before you head home for the night.

Follow these steps to figure out if you should be doing these emails right now, or later:

1. If a message requires no action, either delete it or drag it to your 'done' folder.
2. If you can do a simple reply that takes no more than a couple of minutes, do it there and then, and then delete or drag to your 'done' folder.
3. If it needs a more considered response, schedule it for the first two hours of the next day. In some email applications you can convert emails to tasks. This way you can remove it from your inbox, but still have it on the list for action.

TO-DO LIST FOR TOMORROW

Include things you didn't complete today and schedule them for the right time zones for the next day. Not everything has to be done first thing! But keep in mind that you don't have to take this framework literally if you work differently. The real point of this is to find ways to work with, not against, your natural rhythms so your most important work is done during your most productive hours, rather than by default.

» Schedule things that require higher levels of intensity and are impactful first thing in the first two hours.

» Schedule catch-ups, meetings, responses to other people's needs in the second two hours.

» Anything that is repetitive or routine, and that doesn't require high levels of intensity, schedule for the third two hours.

» Follow-ups, planning meetings, and document reviews are all good for the afternoon, so schedule them for the fourth two hours.

GET CLOSURE

One of the last things I do in the afternoon is double-check what I have going on the next day. This way if I have forgotten to prep something, or need to take certain things with me, I can do it then, or decide if I have the time in the morning. If this means I stay back a little longer for a sense of closure or completion, then I do that.

What I don't want to do is wake up in the middle of the night suddenly freaking out about an appointment or meeting that I have forgotten, or need to prepare something for.

Wrapping things up or feeling like things are under control means you will enjoy your evening, and get a much better night's sleep.

DECIDE NOW FOR TOMORROW

Make any small and low-impact decisions today that can clear the way for tomorrow. It could be things like:

» Deciding where and how I will have a discussion—for example, will we go for a walk, go to the downstairs coffee shop, or stay at my desk or their desk?

» Blocking out what time tomorrow's lunch break will be.

» Setting email responders if I'm going to be away or unavailable.

» Changing the message on my voicemail if I'm not available and want to let people know.

» Packing my bag with things I might need: for example, if I am giving a presentation, make sure I have my cables, remote control slide mover, and so on, all ready to go.

» Printing any handouts and documents that I may need the next day.

» Deciding, if tomorrow is a non-routine kind of day,

    – what time I will need to leave in the morning

    – how I will be travelling the next day

    – what train/tram I will catch, or, if driving, what route I will take.

Deciding all these things before you leave the office at night will eliminate any chance of you sitting bolt upright in the middle of the night because you've remembered you need to do 'something'! This also frees you of making these mundane decisions in the morning, which could affect your productivity and state of mind.

Sleep on it

When I do a jigsaw puzzle, there's usually a point in the evening where I stop making much progress. It feels like a struggle, and yet, the next day when I sit down to have a go, I find a piece sitting adjacent to the puzzle and immediately see the place it goes. Or, even worse, it's sitting on the table, right next to the place it goes in the puzzle.

This also happened when writing this book. I would set targets for each day, and, although I would usually write in the last two hours of the day, often if I was struggling with something I would find it much easier to write about the next morning.

It's interesting how we see the end of the day as a time to aim towards finishing things.

Too often we rush to get something done before we finish the workday, when it's best to conclude it the next day, with a fresh mind, after a good sleep.

The idea of 'sleeping on it' was first recorded in the 1500s by Henry VIII in one of his state papers: 'His Grace ... sayd thatt he wold slepe and drem apon the matter.'

When you have a problem or issue, if you sleep on it, you are allowing your unconscious to be involved in the problem-solving process.

Susan Kuchinskas, who writes for WebMD, says that the rapid eye movement (REM) stage of sleep helps us organise and link facts we have accumulated in novel ways.

For example, say you're at an impasse in communicating with a colleague. At night, our brain's hippocampus shuts down and information is moved to the neocortex, where all our other information is stored, and it is then available to be connected to other things. Suddenly, a 'bridge' in your mind is crossed and the answer to the problem appears.

The sparks of creativity come when our neocortex has the opportunity to integrate new information, and associate it with other memories or thoughts.

I leverage this all the time. I will often write down a problem on a note just before I go to sleep, then I pay attention to what I'm thinking when I wake first thing in the morning.

Bottom line, you have more clarity about the problem and will therefore be able to consider the solution.

So rather than sending that angry email at the close of the day, pause and think. There is zero net gain, as it's likely the receiver won't see it until the morning anyway.

Is it Friday?

My client Robyn always blocks out Fridays from 3 pm to 8 pm in her diary. She does this for several reasons.

» It prevents people from taking that time, and she is in control of when she's finished for the day.

» It's time for her to reflect on what she did during the week and score herself on her productivity and outcomes.

» She looks to the coming week and makes some decisions about her key outcomes for the next week.

» She can complete any quick tasks that would give her a kick start for next week.

Taking a leaf out of Robyn's book, you could:

» **Plan your week on a Friday afternoon.** Or, if you must, a Sunday evening. Either way, don't wait until Monday morning. Chances are you will get distracted or caught up in the latest, most urgent thing that is all-consuming that day.

» **Identify your three biggest ticket items.** What are the three things that will give you the greatest return on your investment of time and energy for the week? Schedule these as early as possible, in the first two hours of the day at the start of the week.

» **Overestimate how long things will take.** Don't fall for the 'Planning Fallacy', which is a phenomenon described by Daniel Kahneman and Amos Tversky that says we have an optimism bias when it comes to thinking about the time it will take to complete future tasks. Worst-case scenario is that you have blocked 90 minutes for something that takes you 40 and you have a bit of precious time back.

» **Schedule everything that's important.** Don't leave time in your diary blank, thinking 'That's when I'll catch up on reading'. If catching up on reading is important to note as a task, then block time for 'reading'. (Likely in the third two hours of the day.)

End Friday right and you'll set yourself up for a successful week ahead.

Last 2 minutes

The fourth two hours is about maximising your second wind before logging off for the night.

The momentum you create here will be felt in the first two hours of the next day. More importantly, it will free you up to go home and spend time with your family and friends. All of which gives you the best possible opportunity to start the next day with vigour and motivation.

Working this way gets you out of the vicious cycle of exhaustion, stress and inefficiency and into the positive cycle of energy, enthusiasm and productivity.

It may take a few weeks to reap the benefits but, believe me, when you start working this way you will feel so much more in control of the important things in your life.

TIMING TIP

Give yourself permission to try new things, even if they feel extremely unfamiliar or uncomfortable. The more things you try, the more opportunities you have to find what works for you.

Wear your success

Before bed my friend Rosie always decides what she is wearing and eating the next day, otherwise she just can't sleep.

She chooses an outfit, including shoes and handbag, and hangs it all at the end of her closet, closest to where she gets dressed.

She prepares her lunch and has it ready in the fridge to collect before leaving for work.

Rosie claims it's her secret to success when it comes to being productive!

Another friend, Iris, takes wardrobe planning to a whole other level. She checks the weather forecast and makes her wardrobe decisions for the whole week. She says that sometimes, on a particular day, she will change her mind because she feels like wearing something other than what she's planned, but that's rare, and there still isn't any agonising over the decision. She's got a fallback.

On a Sunday afternoon, my friend Jeremy plans the dinners for the week. With two teenage kids, he likes to have it all organised so that it's either quick for him to make when he gets home, or it's easy for one of the kids to prepare.

All of these folks say that these simple habits have a huge impact on their mental wellbeing and productivity throughout the week.

EXPERIMENT 7

Think about all the things you need to do tomorrow, and in the coming week. Don't forget to include meetings and preparation for those meetings.

Put them into the template shown in figure 7.3 according to the best time of day to be doing them. You can also go to www.thefirst2hours.com.au and download the template.

Now go and block the time in your calendar accordingly.

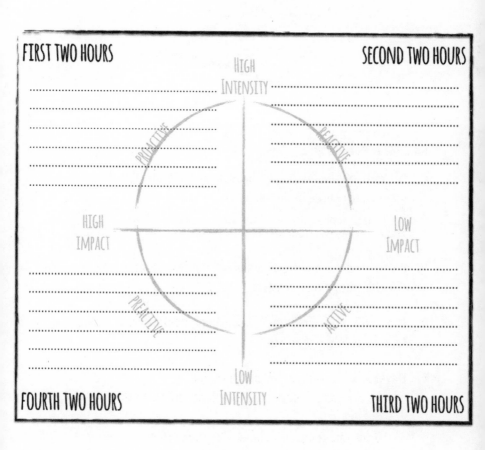

Figure 7.3: planning template

Maximise your fourth 2 hours.

» 'Tick off' all the things you have achieved and enjoy that momentary surge of dopamine!

» Make as many routine decisions as you can for the next day.

» If you haven't already, take a break before getting started on the afternoon home stretch.

» Draft any important things, such as presentations or emails, for review in the morning.

» Develop some rituals that support you:
  — Be disciplined about the time that you will knock off for the day.
  — Until you get to zero, have a Personal Best (PB) for how few emails are left in your inbox.
  — Give yourself a mental pat on the back.

Your First 2 Hours clock

I frequently enjoy holidays on some of the best beaches in the world, in Queensland, Australia. Despite always swimming between the flags, sometimes I can still be overwhelmed by the regularity and size of the waves. I will think that I have successfully navigated a wave, then another one surges over me. It gets exhausting after a while, as I have to maintain high levels of vigilance to avoid getting swamped! Can you relate?

I always admire the surfers, who get beyond the breaks and choose which waves will give them the best ride. They always look so relaxed, sitting out there on their boards.

I reckon our workdays can feel a bit like this: endless waves of demands that we need to negotiate in order to keep our heads above water. We need to be more like surfers, deciding on the right wave at the right time to get the best ride.

So, now that you've read about how your workday could be, rather than being at the mercy of others' demands, it's time to actually design it and do it!

Stop the vicious cycle of overwhelm, tiredness and stalled productivity and start working with your natural rhythms and demands.

Use the template in figure C, or download it from www.thefirst2hours.com.au and work out the best times for you to do the right work at the right time.

Stick the clock above your desk and refer to it throughout the day—you won't regret it.

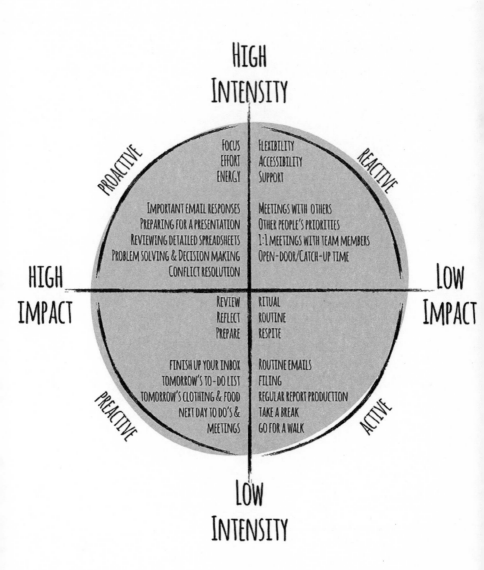

Figure C: your First 2 Hours clock

Work with me

Thank you for reading *The First 2 Hours*.

My intention and hope for writing this book was to give you some alternative ways of thinking about how you can manage your time and be more productive.

My greatest joy would be to see your copy of this book dog-eared, marked, tagged and full of notes and highlights. A book that you have on your desk at work to remind you every day that you are designing your day and are fully in control. That you are giving yourself the best chance to be at your most productive.

If that's what your copy looks like, post a picture of it on the Facebook page:

www.facebook.com/thefirst2hours

Head over to www.thefirst2hours.com.au, where we have a load of free templates, tips and other tools to support you.

And don't forget to drop me a note to let me know how you're progressing.

When I'm not enjoying tea on my verandah, you will find me at the front of the training room working with managers to help them make work *work*. So, if you think you or your team could use a dose of Donna to get things moving along, get in touch for a plan of action.

Thanks again!

Donna

d@donnamcgeorge.com
www.donnamcgeorge.com
Facebook: www.facebook.com/makingworkwork
LinkedIn: donnamcgeorge
Twitter: @dmcgeorge

Sources

Introduction

I Done This blog, 'Quiz: What Productivity Personality Are You? How to Maximize Your Productivity in 2017'. http://blog.idonethis.com/productivity-quiz/

Chapter 1

Smolensky, M and Lambert, L (2000). *The Body Clock Guide to Better Health: How to Use Your Body's Natural Clock to Fight Illness and Achieve Maximum Health*. Henry Holt and Company.

Deloitte, (2017). 'UK public are "glued to smartphones" as device adoption reaches new heights'. https://www2.deloitte.com/uk/en/pages/press-releases/articles/uk-public-glued-to-smartphones.html

Wansink, B and Sobal, J (2007). 'Mindless eating: The 200 daily food decisions we overlook'. *Environment and Behavior*, 39(1): 106–23.

Chen, J et al., (2016). 'Oh What a Beautiful Morning! Diurnal variations in executives' and analysts' behavior: Evidence from conference calls'. *Management Science*. https://doi.org/10.1287/mnsc.2017.2888

Dodds, PS et al., (2011). 'Temporal patterns of happiness and Information in a global social network: Hedonometrics and Twitter'. *PLOS One*, 6(12): e26752.

Stone, AA et al., (2006). 'A population approach to the study of emotion: diurnal rhythms of a working day examined with the Day Reconstruction Method'. *Emotion*, 6(1): 139–49.

Horne, JA and Östberg, O, (1976). 'A self-assessment questionnaire to determine morningness-eveningness in human circadian rhythms'. *International Journal of Chronobiology*, 4: 97–110.

Danziger, S et al., (2011). 'Extraneous factors in judicial decisions'. Proceedings of the National Academy of Sciences of the United States of America, 108(17): 6889–92.

Pink, D (2018). *When: The Scientific Secrets of Perfect Timing*. Riverhead Books.

Chapter 2

Conner, TS et al., (2015). 'On carrots and curiosity: eating fruit and vegetables is associated with greater flourishing in daily life.' *British Journal of Health Psychology*, 20(2): 413–27.

Institute of Medicine; Food and Nutrition Board; Committee on Military Nutrition Research, (1994). *Food Components to Enhance Performance: An Evaluation of Potential Performance-Enhancing Food Components for Operational Rations*.

Coulson, JC, et al., (2008). 'Exercising at work and self-reported work performance'. *International Journal of Workplace Health Management*, 1(3): 176–97.

Garber, CE, et al., (2011). 'Quantity and quality of exercise for developing and maintaining cardiorespiratory, musculoskeletal, and neuromotor fitness in apparently healthy adults: Guidance for prescribing exercise'. *Medicine and Science in Sports and Exercise*, 43(7): 1334–59.

Lavelle, P, (2010). 'Study proves exercise boosts immune system'. ABC Science. http://www.abc.net.au/science/articles/2010/11/02/3054621.htm

ten Brinke, LF, et al., (2015). 'Aerobic exercise increases hippocampal volume in older women with probable mild cognitive impairment: A 6-month randomized controlled trial'. *British Journal of Sports Medicine*, 49(4): 248–54.

Williamson, AM and Feyer, A-M, (2000). 'Moderate sleep deprivation produces impairments in cognitive and motor performance equivalent to legally prescribed levels of alcohol intoxication'. *Occupational and Environmental Medicine*, 57(10): 649–55.

Dinges, D et al., (1997). 'Cumulative sleepiness, mood disturbance, and psychomotor vigilance performance decrements during a week of sleep restricted to 4–5 hours per night'. *Sleep*, 20(4): 267–77.

Pencavel, J, (2014). 'The productivity of working hours April 2014'. Institute for the Study of Labor (IZA), Discussion Paper Series.

Palmer, F, (2017). 'Checking your phone before bed is seriously damaging your health'. *Marie Claire*. https://www .marieclaire.co.uk/life/health-fitness/mobile-phone-health -affects-512005

Chapter 3

Napier, NK, (2014). 'The myth of multitasking'. *Psychology Today*. https://www.psychologytoday.com/us/blog/creativity -without-borders/201405/the-myth-multitasking

SWNS, (2017). 'Americans check their phones 80 times a day: Study'. *NY Post*. https://nypost.com/2017/11/08/americans -check-their-phones-80-times-a-day-study/

Kahneman, D, (2011). *Thinking, Fast and Slow*. Farrar, Straus and Giroux.

Fox, J, (2014). *The Game Changer*. John Wiley & Sons.

Perham, N and Vizard, J, (2011). 'Can preference for background music mediate the irrelevant sound effect?' *Applied Cognitive Psychology*, 25(4): 625–31.

Chapter 4

DMR, (2018). '90 interesting email statistics and facts (2018)'. https://expandedramblings.com/index.php/email-statistics/

Baer, D, (2013). 'Why 80 percent of your emails are a total waste'. *fast company*. https://www.fastcompany.com/3015643 /why-80-percent-of-your-emails-are-a-total-waste

Crowley, D, (2015). *Smart Work*. John Wiley & Sons.

Chapter 5

Heifetz, R, (1994). *Leadership without Easy Answers*. Belknap Press: Harvard University Press.

Kruse, K, (2016). 'Why successful leaders don't have an open door policy'. *Forbes*. https://www.forbes.com/sites/kevinkruse/2016/04/24/why-successful-leaders-dont-have-an-open-door-policy/#1dab52931ef7

Chapter 6

Loughborough University, (2013). 'Email — yet more stress at the office?'. Press release, PR 13/98. https://www.lboro.ac.uk/media-centre/press-releases/2013/june/email—yet-more-stress-at-the-office.html

Barley, SR et al., (2011). 'E-mail as a source and symbol of Stress'. *Organization Science*, 22(4): 887–906.

Huffington, A, (2017). 'How to keep email from ruining your vacation'. *Harvard Business Review*. https://hbr.org/2017/08/how-to-keep-email-from-ruining-your-vacation

Holz, J et al., (2012). 'The timing of learning before night-time sleep differentially affects declarative and procedural long-term memory consolidation in adolescents'. *PLOS One*, 7(7): e40963.

di Cagno, A et al., (2013). 'Time of day — Effects on motor coordination and reactive strength in elite athletes and untrained adolescents'. *Journal of Sports Science & Medicine*, 12(1): 182–189.

Gawande, A, (2009). *The Checklist Manifesto*. Henry Holt and Company.

Thøgersen-Ntoumani, C et al., (2015). 'Changes in work affect in response to lunchtime walking in previously physically inactive employees: A randomized trial'. *Scandinavian Journal of Medicine & Science in Sports*, 25(6): 778–87.

Walker, M, (2017). *Why We Sleep: The New Science of Sleep and Dreams*. Penguin.

Pink, D, (2018). *When: The Scientific Secrets of Perfect Timing*. Riverhead Books.

Chapter 7

Condor, B, (1994). 'The body clock', *Chicago Tribune*. https://www.chicagotribune.com/news/ct-xpm-1994-10-31-9410310028-story.html

Kuchinskas, S, (2010). 'Got a problem? Try sleeping on it'. https://www.webmd.com/mental-health/features/need-to-solve-a-problem-try-sleeping-on-it#1

Kahneman, D and Tversky, A, (1977). 'Intuitive prediction: Biases and corrective procedures'. Decision Research Technical Report PTR-1042-77-6.

Index